# THE FIRE WITHIN

*Lessons from defeat that have inspired a passion for learning*

Compiled and edited by
## Mandy Froehlich

The Fire Within
Mandy Froehlich

Published by EduMatch®
PO Box 150324, Alexandria, VA 22315
www.edumatch.org

© 2018 Mandy Froehlich
All rights reserved. No portion of this book may be reproduced in any form without permission from the publisher, except as permitted by U.S. copyright law. For permissions contact sarah@edumatch.org.

These books are available at special discounts when purchased in quantity for use as premiums, promotions fundraising, and educational use. For inquiries and details, contact the publisher: sarah@edumatch.org.

Names have been changed to protect the privacy of individuals mentioned.

ISBN-13: 978-1-7322487-1-7
ISBN-10: 1-7322487-1-0

# Dedication

There are goals that we set for ourselves in life, and then there are the ones that we were meant to do, the ones that seem to have been made for us. This book has been the latter. Usually, I find when that happens it is accompanied by feelings of uncertainty and inadequacy to complete what you were called to accomplish. Thankfully, I had friends and family that supported me in this crazy endeavor without fail. Like my daughter who called upon her friends when I couldn't come up with an idea I liked for the cover art, which her 15-year-old friend, Erin, ended up designing on Snapchat. I couldn't have asked for better support and understanding when my patience was thin from the inevitable writer's block. So, to Dan and my kids Brycen, Tyler, Cortlynne and Addisyn, my superheroes, my dear friends and PLF, my mentors, the contributors and poets, Kevin Honeycutt for gifting me some of his bravery, and my publisher Sarah for believing in me, thank you from the deepest depths of my heart.

# Table of Contents

Preface .................................................................................. 1
Foreword ............................................................................... 3
Beginning with the End ........................................................ 9
The Girl & Her Little Red Suitcase ..................................... 23
Broken Perception ............................................................... 39
Victim to Advocate: One Teacher's Story ......................... 51
The Power Within ............................................................... 65
From Adversity to Art ......................................................... 75
Out of the Darkness ............................................................ 99
Career Atrophy and Healing Process Driven by Two Index Fingers .................................................................. 111
Dueling the Parent and Educator Role as an EDvocate ................................................................................ 127
Overcomer Teacher ........................................................... 141
Educator of Steel ............................................................... 155
Courage Over Fear ............................................................ 173
The Deep-Reaching Effects of Trauma ........................... 193
After the Storm: Secondary Trauma and Post-Traumatic Growth .............................................................................. 215
Control Your Ending ........................................................ 225
Honorary Mention Student Poetry Submissions .......... 237
About Mandy ..................................................................... 255

# Preface

> *"Happiness can be found in the darkest of times, if one only remembers to turn on the light."*
> Albus Dumbledore, Harry Potter and the Prisoner of Azkaban

This project began as a tiny spark of an idea that I had while traveling home from ISTE in 2017. I was sitting on the flight next to my good friend Tara Martin, and we were exchanging our "why we decided on education as our calling" stories. There were some differences in our paths, but still enough similarities that for the first time in my whole life I didn't feel like I was the only person to have had experiences like mine. At first, I was relieved to not feel so alone. Then, I was angry that I was so embarrassed by my past that I didn't feel like I could talk about it. I knew there had to be more people who felt like I did, and decided to go on a hunt for people brave enough to tell their stories and reflective enough to know how their experiences made them a better teacher for their students. I was positive there were more of us. I just needed to find them, and I did. You'll see them as the contributors to this book and feel the input from so many other unseen members who weren't quite ready to be so public with their stories.

Eleven stories of traumatic experiences are told from the perspective of eleven people. It's important to note that these very personal stories are told from their angle, and although perspective is always someone's reality, it may not have been another's in that same situation. It is not the intent of any of the contributors to vilify anyone in their stories. Our goal has been to be brave enough to share our defeats in order for others to feel comfortable to share theirs, to hope they know they're not alone, and to give them the fortitude to either help themselves or others as they work through their own struggles.

# Foreword

*Bethany Hill*

As educators, we interact with people every day who have various backgrounds and social histories that make up a story. Our focus is on kids, and we are charged with bringing our very best to the profession. When we have bad days, kids are not supposed to feel it. Our attitudes and dispositions have a direct impact on the climate of a classroom and school. As I read Mandy's words, I was reminded of the tremendous responsibility we have each day to ensure we bring encouragement and inspiration to those around us. We are accountable to so many...students, colleagues, our administrators, families, the community...they are all watching us. We are expected to enter the doors of our schools and leave everything behind for the school day. We have stories, and many of them paint periods of hurt, sadness, fear, anxiety, and trauma. Every day we see children come to school with so much in their emotional backpacks, and sometimes they unleash all of it on us. We do not judge, and we do not waiver. WE are the strong ones because THEY need US. Our emotional backpacks were checked at the door and will be waiting on us when the day ends. What a challenge this is, and there are times where we may fall short of separating our personal struggles with our professional days. How do we balance?

People evolve through their circumstances and are molded from their life experiences. We can be a product of our circumstances, or we can rise above them to empowerment. Throughout *The Fire Within*, there are stories of people who overcame their circumstances of trauma, mental health, and emotional dysregulation. The educators who share their heartfelt experiences have demonstrated the ultimate level of vulnerability. We are in the sweet spot of learning and growth when we are in a state of disequilibrium. This emotional state is not comfortable, but as you read through the raw emotions shared in the following pages, you will see that these people are prevailing from adversity in their past. Passion speaks to people. Our past experiences feed directly into our ability to grow passionate about something. There is no time like the present for our passion to be revealed.

As educators, we serve as counselors, nurses, parents, friends, mentors, and so much more. What if we used our own stories to become the person kids come back to and share the difference we made? What if our fire within blazed out of control for our own self-care and healing as we serve others in the process? Every school day is a new opportunity to color a child's soul. Our own evolution with self-care, healing from adverse experiences in our past, and choosing to prevail rather than to fall victim will maximize our potential to help others discover the fire within them.

The sun rises and sets every single day. What we do in between is up to us. We can go through the motions pushing our stories aside, or we can disrupt our own thinking and use our stories to impact those around us.

Your fire within is a catalyst for igniting one in others...that is the message I am taking away from this

## FOREWORD
## BETHANY HILL

book. Pay it forward and let the fuel for your own fire come back to you. It is an act of reciprocity like no other, and it will keep our flame eternal.

# PART I
# Our Stories

***you flame***
*By Courtney Fuso (age 13)*

*why pretend to be water,
for someone who is too afraid to handle
being stepped on,
that flame that continues to grow,
from every single blow,
every single throw,
you feel an afterglow,
igniting inside,
you overcame,
you flame.*

# Chapter One

# Beginning with the End

*Mandy Froehlich*

> *"Something very beautiful happens to people when their world has fallen apart; a humility, a nobility, a higher intelligence emerges at just the point when our knees hit the floor."*
> -Marianne Williamson

It's always at the end when everything before becomes clear. The reason for heartache, distress, and anxiety can be seen. The decisions that might have been different had you only known what was about to happen. Hindsight being 20/20, and all that. Going through a difficult time, an adversity, can be like that. It's only at the end when you've relentlessly worked through the multitude of internal struggles that you can see the silver linings.

One of my most fundamental life beliefs is that our stories and our life experiences shape who we are. Every decision, reaction, or relationship we have or create is directed and defined by our past experiences and how we have reacted to the adversity that has happened in our lives. Our stories can be so powerful that they can dictate all future interactions, and our reactions to them can be either detrimental to our well-being or inspirational and motivational to the people around us.

Sometimes, they are a combination of the two, and we continue our struggles while we work for the good of others.

People always show their true character in the moments when life gets difficult. It's not adversity itself that defines a person; it's how they react to the situation. Every reaction is a choice we make. Sometimes people choose to live in the darkness of sorrow and hurt, to carry that with them and allow it to spur on anger and resentment or use it as reason to hurt other people the way they've been hurt. But others find their way through the darkness and use their experience as a springboard for helping others find their way as well, whether it be counselors, doctors and nurses, or as in our case, educators.

## The Teacher's Heart

Being in the education profession is a unique experience. Educators are required to bring their best selves to work every day. They are expected to exude normalcy, positivity, and self-control even in the face of meltdowns, angry parents, and active shooter drills. They need to be mentally and emotionally strong to not only be in a room with thirty or more kids every day, but also to create opportunities for their students to learn and grow, build their character, teach them personal hygiene and internet safety, how to tie their shoes, and how to make it through their own adversities even stronger than we've made it through ours.

The ability to be a mentor, supporter, and counselor on a regular basis, every single day no matter what, comes from their teacher's heart. It's that feeling when a kid has a lightbulb moment, or when a child with difficult behaviors seems happy instead of angry, or when a student comes back to your classroom years later and says, "Remember when we did _____ in class? That was awesome."

It is the combination of moments and feelings that you can only get from working with students, hearing them laugh, and watching them triumph over struggles. Those are the moments that keep teachers pushing through when also dealing with new initiatives, rules made by government officials that have never been in a classroom as an educator, and a constant underlying threat of violence. The act of staying in a challenging profession is a choice that teachers make because of the reward of working with children and the desire to be the difference that places students on the right path.

It's a difficult profession, but it's the challenge that makes it great. If teaching were easy, everyone would do it. Educators, in general, need to have special skills and talents to do what they do. Sometimes those superpowers need to support kids who go home to a difficult life or have had experiences that have created challenges that carry over into the classroom. There is nothing easy about being a teacher, but there is something special about teaching. The second we forget our teacher's heart, it will become significantly more difficult to remember why we teach to begin with, and kids deserve better than that.

Many of us have gone into education to make a difference of some kind. For some people, it's because they had a teacher who made a difference in their lives, or possibly a parent was a teacher, and they lived with the dedication that the education profession requires. It might have been that they knew it was their calling and they spent many of their childhood days teaching their stuffed animals their ABCs and addition. However, for some people, our life experiences have revealed education to be our passion and spurred us on. For others, our experiences have focused us on certain areas that are special to us because of adversity we have experienced in our past.

While stories of adversity are often sensationalized by the media for sports figures and musicians, educators need to be cognizant of the fact that they work with children and anything that could make them seem "different" might make them a target. Also, because teachers are expected to maintain as much normalcy as possible, it might seem as though we are the only ones that are struggling with issues because everyone around us seems to have their lives together. Yet sometimes it's our daily struggles that give us the extra edge to do our jobs extraordinarily well.

Teachers often don't like to share our stories of adversity because we feel like we need to be strong for the little people we work with. Often it is our struggles that give us strengths that are unique to us and support our work with others. We don't want to be looked at differently by parents or colleagues because just by being a teacher, we are held to different standards than other professions, and we don't want to haul around our baggage for everyone to see. Sometimes, it's just that our adversity has caused us to desire a place where we can feel normal and accepted, and possibly looked at like we belong. When people don't know our past, it allows us to build our future and have a place where we can live outside our own heads. For these reasons, educators don't typically advertise the difficulties they've lived through.

By nature, teachers are typically humble characters. They don't get into education for the pay or recognition, or to be told they're great. That being said, there are times when it's important to recognize your strengths. First, taking the time to identify your strengths means you also recognize your weaknesses, and it's as important to know one as it is the other. Second, knowing what you excel at allows you to be aware of what you bring to the table when you collaborate with others and use your powers for good. So many times, I work with teachers who are bashful when I ask them what their strengths are because they don't want to toot their own horn, but there is definitely a difference between bragging and being willing to recognize your talents and share your ideas. Being humble and sharing your strengths are not mutually exclusive. In fact, as an educator, it's imperative that we recognize those strengths and use them in our work with children. It's our duty. It has taken me a long time and a significant amount of effort to come to this realization because I've found that in general, we learn about our strengths and weaknesses best from going through a challenging situation. True reflection contains some personal and/or professional soul-searching. No matter how we come by

13

these realizations, it's time that we all start to wear what we know to be our great qualities at as a badge of honor, so we can continue learning in the areas where we haven't earned our badges yet.

## Education and Mental Health Issues

Education has gotten better at recognizing mindfulness and mental health. We take brain breaks, practice yoga in classrooms and we teach deep breathing exercises to kids. We have started to recognize the importance of mental health for teachers as well and have begun to teach them mindfulness strategies as well as tips for dealing with secondary trauma and stress. But for our mental health to be optimal, we need to also recognize mental health issues, and nobody wants to talk about that. We want to work on getting people mentally healthy without recognizing that some people need additional help and support beyond Downward Dog.

It's a challenge for some to recognize these issues because you can't see the parts that are broken from the outside. They are not physically obvious like a broken bone or sprained ankle; there are no casts or braces. Because of the nature of our profession, many of us are fantastic at hiding the issues with smiles and fake cheerfulness which seems genuine because we have had a ridiculous amount of practice at making it that way.

Like many other survivors of trauma, I suffer from depression and anxiety. There are so many common misunderstandings about both challenges, and because of that, we try to keep those feelings bottled up, so we don't look "weird."

## BEGINNING WITH THE END
## MANDY FROEHLICH

Depression is not about choosing to feel happy or sad, choosing to smile or be serious. Anxiety is not about just being nervous. Nobody would choose to have these kinds of feelings if they could help it. I have depression and anxiety.

For me, it's like having a disconnect between the logical side and the emotional side of my brain. My emotional brain is my biggest, most effective and dangerous bully. It tells me every morning that I'm fat and worthless, that I've done nothing with my life and I matter to no one. It tells me that the world would be a better place without me and that although other people tell me it would be selfish, I would actually be doing a service to the people, so they didn't have to "put up" with me. My logical brain tells me that part of my brain is defective, and I should ignore it, and I hold onto logic like a life raft to get me through tough moments.

Minute by minute, I work through my days. I focus on breathing in and breathing out because I sometimes find that I'm holding my breath. I tell myself that if I can get through one minute, I can get through the next. I have a difficult time compartmentalizing simple things because I work so hard to keep this part of myself under lock and key. I sometimes sit at my desk and cry when everyone else has left the office because I am exhausted from all the effort of just trying to be someone better than myself. In my darkest times, I feel like I have more than a broken heart, I have a broken soul. Yet I get up every day, go to work, put on a smile, and work with and for our kids, serving and supporting the people around me. I use humor as a defense mechanism. Sometimes the happier

I seem, the more depressed I actually am, which really just perpetuates the perception that I'm ok. The fact that not many people would know this about me is always a personal win.

For me, depression is also not a one-time occurrence. I have lived with it every day for at least 25 years. Sometimes I am on an upswing, and I have it under control. Sometimes there is a trigger that sets it off, sometimes it happens for no apparent reason. The idea that depression goes away or is just about being sad are fallacies. I often think of my upswing times as just being in remission.

I get through these times with a strong support system. I have people around me who believe in me for me when I don't believe in myself. Some know me so well they can sense it, which is so important because it's difficult to talk about. It's seen as a weakness, and people say, "How can you not be happy? You've been successful, you have great kids, you smile and laugh...I saw you do it! You'll be fine! Just think happy thoughts." And that's what my logical brain would tell me, but my emotional brain fights it, and I need my people to keep me afloat until I'm able to do it again myself.

We are often told that we need to leave our personal issues in the car when we come to work, and I totally agree with this 100%. Depression and/or anxiety is not an excuse for dumping our problems on our students or the people around us. Our students have enough on their plates. They do not need the personal issues of adults added to them. That is incredibly unfair to do to them. That means, however, for people who are dealing with true mental health issues like depression or anxiety, our ability to hide our feelings is of the utmost importance. It is not optional. It is imperative that our students and colleagues get only the best versions of us, even if it is temporarily not the real one. We do need to teach our students about mental health issues and be transparent with what we are working through, but that is different than allowing our mental health issues to affect our students negatively.

So many educators I've spoken with who have these same issues have felt a connection with people like Robin Williams. Other depressed individuals who have put everyone else's happiness before their own lost their battle because they had nothing left for themselves to deal with their own demons. Think of any great educator you know, and they would fit the mold of someone who gives themselves over to the people they surround themselves with, and you may never know the internal battle that's raging. We have people around us every day who need additional support, and we may never know it because they are doing the best they can for the people around them.

I recognize that even making a choice to write about my feelings on depression and mental health issues is going out on a limb. Many people don't want to read or acknowledge the truths behind how someone with these afflictions might feel. But I don't want people who are suffering from these ailments to feel like they suffer in a dark corner alone like I have so many times.

When confessing to people in the past, I've watched their facial expressions turn from one of caring to one of either pity or concern that I might be "unstable," and I worry that their uninformed reasoning might result in them questioning my ability to work with kids. I want others to know that they are not weird or crazy (a super irritating word for someone with true mental illness), even though they may feel like people are looking at them that way when they speak about it. I want people to recognize that mental health is more than just showing people how to reduce stress, but it is also about recognizing mental illness and supporting people when and where they need it most. I want the lucky ones who haven't felt this way to empathize and to understand that there is nothing on Earth I'd love more than to not feel sad. Stop telling me to smile and trust me when I say I'm trying so hard, just like anyone else dealing with these same issues.

## Trauma and the Brain

Our stories of adversity do have the potential to have caused us trauma. Depression, post-traumatic stress disorder (PTSD), anxiety, and a host of other fallouts from trauma that can linger for years, if not a lifetime.

One of the more important aspects of trauma to understand is that it physiologically changes the way the brain functions. These issues have had so much social stigma attached to them for so long that it is difficult for people, especially those who work with children, to be willing to admit to those challenges. However, an important aspect of ending the stigma and providing understanding is to understand the science behind trauma.

So, what happens when an adult with trauma is working with a student who has had a similar experience? How does the brain change when faced with a traumatic event? How does repeated trauma cause the brain to think differently? Knowing the answers will give us insight as to how the support we either need or provide may look different than the typical mindfulness techniques. The answers to these questions will be provided in Chapter 13: *The Deep Reaching Effects of Trauma.*

## The Fire Within

This book is a compilation of personal stories of adversity by educators who have gone through extraordinary circumstances and have come through stronger and have taken their new strengths into the classroom to work with students or into leadership positions to support teachers. The stories are inspirational and sometimes heartbreaking but written with the intention to motivate others and ensure that others going through adversity won't feel alone. During our darkest times, we can develop skills and characteristics that make us exceptional, similar to suffering through a spider bite to become a superhero. Except educators save the world by working with our children.

The purpose of this book is twofold. First, during those dark times, we can feel like we are completely alone- especially in today's world of social media where it appears that everyone has a perfectly put together life; both our past adversities and our current ones can alienate us from others by creating a feeling like we are different. And frankly, we are, and that's what makes us special. However, while dealing with adversity, it's possible to forget the light that can come from even the darkest of places. Only after you've been through it can you look back and understand the why. This book is to remind others who may be suffering that they are not alone, and that especially in the field of education, the characteristics we develop due to adversity can support the people around us. We have gravitated toward the field of education for a purpose: to make a difference. Our superpowers allow us to make that difference, and other people have suffered trauma and heartbreak and have become amazing educators and leaders because (or in spite) of it.

The second purpose of this book is to give a glimpse into the worlds that any student in any class might be experiencing. I was recently speaking with a teacher who told me in her previous district the teachers would gather Thanksgiving supplies for their neediest families and bring them to their homes, so they could have a good meal on that night. She told me that there was no way to prepare for the first time that she visited a run-down, dilapidated mobile home of one of her students.

Reasoning through what you think your students endure and actually experiencing it through their eyes are two totally different things. Any story in this book could be one of the students in your class. The stories might be difficult for you to read. Imagine how it is for the child who is living it, and now think about how you might help that child meet both their most basic needs and help them grow and learn. Their experiences will make them who they are, just as our experiences have shaped us. It is our duty as educators, to understand our children's deepest needs beyond their education, and some of our students are living lives that some of us can't even imagine.

Following the stories of our servant superheroes is a chapter on trauma and the brain, post-traumatic growth, secondary trauma, and coping mechanisms for dealing with trauma as an adult. There is a common hope from all the authors that readers will feel empowered, inspired, and will focus on recognizing the strengths that they bring to their students, as well as have strategies for dealing with either past or future adversity and trauma.

# Chapter Two
# The Girl & Her Little Red Suitcase

*Mandy Froehlich*

> *"It's okay if you fall down and lose your spark.
> Just make sure that when you get up,
> you rise as the whole damn fire."*
> -Colette Werden

Mandy Froehlich is first and foremost an educator, but also a Director of Innovation & Technology, speaker & consultant. Networking and working with others in the field of education on leadership, professional development, student-driven learning, and innovation are her passions, and she can be reached via her website at www.mandyfroehlich.com or on Twitter at @froehlichm.

I remember standing on the front porch. I must've been about five years old this time, but it had happened on multiple occasions, so I'm never really sure. The fact of the matter is I have nearly no memory of my childhood, and I prefer it this way. I have just little flashes here and there in no particular order. In this scene, when I reimagine it, it's always pouring rain. But in real life, I don't think it actually was. I was pounding on the front door and screaming for my mother to let me in. She had "kicked me out" with my little red suitcase packed and lying by my feet because I had been too excited to see my father that came around only once or twice a year, and I wasn't allowed to be excited for that.

I was hysterical crying, yelling, "Please, just let me back in," and, "I don't actually want to see him," and, "I love you so much." If I didn't say these things, she wouldn't open the door. I might not have known much when I was five, but I knew how to lie to survive. I knew that what I said and what I believed could be two different things if it allowed me to have some semblance of peace, even if just for a short period of time. So, I told her I hated him and that I would do anything she asked, and I would sob huge tears of genuine fear that I would have to go through the ordeal of begging to get into my house again. Of course I would, time and time again, until the day I just left.

My mother was manipulative and extraordinarily cruel. The cruelty came in the form of giving me what appeared to be love and then taking it away, alongside inhumane ways to talk to and treat a child. One moment she'd be singing Another One Bites the Dust with me at the top of her lungs in the car, happy and smiling. The next moment, turning on a dime, she'd be sending me to bed at 5:30pm because she couldn't stand to look at me, or calling me names and telling me that I was her reason for never going to college. I was why she failed. She could have actually been something, but she wasn't, and it was my fault. I was useless. Her mood swings gave me emotional whiplash.

There have been times over the course of my life that I haven't wanted to complain about my childhood because I felt like suffering emotional and verbal abuse with mild physical abuse wasn't as bad as some of the torturous physical abuse that some of my siblings suffered. But as I've gotten older, and I've had to deal with my own demons from my experiences (like my own insatiable need to please everyone and, deep down, make everyone like me, or the absolute crippling fear of being abandoned that I still live with every day), I've come to realize that all kinds of abuse take their own special toll on the victim...that bruises can be on the skin, but they can also be on the heart and in the mind. There are other little flashes of scenes and sounds that I remember. I remember her putting me to bed early and listening to her "be" with her boyfriends. I learned about adult actions and conversations way too early for a little girl to know. I remember some of them beating her. There are some memories that your mind just can't forget.

Some abused kids are labeled as "those kids" in school. The ones that you can pick out a mile away. They're either extremely compliant and submissive, or they act out. They either hang on you with hugs because they don't get it at home, or they don't want to be touched and flinch when you reach for them. The ones we don't usually recognize as quickly (if at all) are the ones who are compliant and submissive because they are always doing what you ask and never causing a ruckus. I was that kid. I didn't need additional drama in my life, I had enough of that at home. I would go to school, do what I knew the teachers expected of me, and go home.

I was unbearably shy in elementary school and did not like talking to adults. When I was in second grade, I peed my pants right in my desk chair. I was too terrified to ask the teacher to go to the bathroom because I didn't want to talk to her, and I didn't know where the bathroom was in my school. I always earned high grades because school came easy to me, and I knew that teachers wouldn't pay me much attention if I just did what I was supposed to do. When I entered middle school and high school, I began to get more social, but I was never allowed to go out and do the things my friends were doing, so eventually, they stopped asking.

I think that one of my breaking points was actually a very small moment in time. My boyfriend in high school, for whatever reason, had been kind enough to give me roses. They were beautiful, and I loved them, and like any other normal person, I took all the little plastic water holders off the bottom of the flowers, threw them in my bathroom garbage, and put the roses in a vase. The next day while I was at school, I received a call from the office that I was to go home immediately with no explanation. I'm not sure that anyone can understand the kind of terror that a kid in my situation feels when something like this happens. It's an all-encompassing shaking, throat-restricting, heart-pounding fear of what might happen.

Not only was the predictability and structure of school the only place I felt truly safe, but I had absolutely no clue what to prepare myself for when I reached my house. Scenarios ran through my head all the way home. She could be crying because of some imaginary way I hurt her, or she could be angry because of her perception of something I did wrong. Calling me home from school was definitely not the norm.

When I entered the house, everything was quiet and still, but a person in this situation learns to never mistake calm for stable. After all, the eye of a hurricane is just an interlude from the rest of the storm. When I saw my mother, she passed me a handful of the roses' water caps and began her tirade. I was silent the entire time as she called me a slut and whore, not quite being able to comprehend what she was talking about. I wasn't even able to defend myself because I didn't know what I was defending myself against. My mind raced, frantically trying to put together the pieces of disjointed information I was getting into anything that would make sense. What was wrong with getting roses? Something that had made me so happy was now ruined, tainted by the vicious accusations that I couldn't find the reason for. Finally, she let me into her mind for the second I needed to figure out what was going on. "How many pregnancy tests did you need to take?"

Never having taken a pregnancy test, I didn't know at the time what they even looked like, but I started sputtering out partial sentences about roses and water and nervously pointing at the beautiful flowers sitting on the cupboard. And just like when a hurricane passes, it was done with an, "Oh."

No apology, no reconciliation for all the horrible things she had just said. I left the house and went back to school, but at that point, I knew my mother was sick. There was something wrong that I wasn't equipped to handle. She often called me selfish and looking back, she might have been right sometimes, but it was my way of coping. I honestly didn't have the capacity to work on keeping myself afloat in the midst of chaos, let alone deal with and support her sickness.

I sometimes wonder if I could have been then who I am now; if I could have had the strength to help her get what she needed to be better, and then maybe I would have the mother that I've always wanted to have. Looking back as an adult, I have still never been able to find what that was about since pregnancy tests and those tubes look nothing alike. But I believe it to just be another one of the ways for her to look for me to fail. If I got pregnant, I would be the slut and whore that she believed me to be, and she would be able to find peace in the fact that I'd have to experience everything I put her through by having my own baby that held me back. But honestly, that's just a guess. Mental illness doesn't live by any rules.

Around this same time, during my Junior year, I became depressed and started falling asleep in class. What always struck me as odd was that when I would wake up, I would always feel guilty because I didn't want the teacher to feel bad, like I would give the impression that their teaching was boring and put me to sleep. But none of my teachers asked me what was wrong.

On my route home from school, there was a big tree at the end of a T in the road, and when I got my license, I used to dream about running my little, gray Geo Metro into it as fast as I could. For years, every time I went down that road, I would floor my gas pedal and slam on the brakes at the last minute like I was playing chicken with the tree. I would fantasize about wrapping my car around the tree, knowing that the impact would crush it like a soda can. I'd imagine what it would look like to see that, to feel like it would feel just to let go and end it all. I wondered if it would hurt, but I doubted it would hurt as much as my life. I wanted it to end so badly, the turmoil, the emotional agony that was so bad that it was actually physically painful...but I could never quite do it. I could never quite keep my foot on the gas pedal long enough to make it happen.

In my early 20's, long after I had ceased communicating with my family, my mother and stepfather were arrested on multiple accounts of child trafficking and abuse for things like telling their biological and adopted kids to dig their own graves and taking away prosthetic limbs as a punishment. At that time, I had family members who were seemingly shocked at the news call me to tell me that they couldn't believe that I didn't tell anyone. How could I not report them?

While I don't think I ever satisfied them with an answer, the truth was that I did. I had told the high school guidance counselor what had been happening at home when I was a senior. It was the same day that a friend of mine had turned me in for being suicidal. The guidance counselor listened to me, told me that I had a very nice family, called my mother, told her what I had said, and then simply sent me home. They agreed that I was an irrational, vindictive teenage girl who was just trying to make my family look bad because I wasn't getting enough attention at home. I never spoke of it to anyone again. If you ever want to stop an abused person from talking about their experience, making them out to be the perpetrator of hurt is definitely the way to do it.

The Fallout

Nearly every time someone finds out about my past, they ask how I turned out so normal. I always laugh and answer the same way every time: normal is relative. I play normal very well, especially on the surface. I think the better questions is how I mentally survived something that many other people don't surface from. That question I actually can't answer. The only information I can give is that even when I was the most hurt by what was happening to me, whether I was crying quietly in my car because I had to let it out or when I would go in my bedroom and scream into my pillow and kick my feet as hard as I could, I knew that what she was doing was wrong. I knew that for as far back as I can remember.

I didn't believe the things she called me even though I internalized them; I never thought I deserved the treatment I got. I knew her issues and illness had nothing to do with me. I never looked at the situation as real life, but rather a matter of survival. When you think something is real, you tend to believe it. When you know you're trying to survive, you believe you can overcome it.

One mistake that people often make when becoming involved with me either personally or professionally is mistaking my ability to act normal as actually feeling that way. The issue with trauma is that while you can learn to cope with your feelings, it never really goes away. You just work to develop the tools to handle the feelings more constructively. I can go through many of my days being busy and pushing down the constant feelings of inadequacy and disconnection that I often still feel. My main coping mechanism has been to use my brain to reason through feelings. Sometimes it works, and sometimes it absolutely doesn't. I often stress eat, which causes weight gain and perpetuates the discomfort I feel in my own body.

I usually feel like my heart and mind are at war. My heart feels the pain that I have experienced from things people have done and said to me, but my brain tries to tell me it's not true. Being told you're worthless and then being shown you're worthless by being abandoned brings on feelings of not being good enough for others and the constant need to prove myself. I'm fortunate that my brain has told me that if I feel I need to be better, I need to learn and grow in that area versus just telling me that I'll never make it. It took me a long time and a lot of practice to get there, to be able to use my mind as the powerful tool it is.

There are still moments where I wonder if I'll ever be good enough personally or professionally, or if I'll ever reach the level I'm striving for. However, being mindful about what I have accomplished, taking moments to look back at how far I've come, and even writing down my goals and checking them off as I go, have helped me to keep my feelings in check. I've found it helpful to actually celebrate little accomplishments before setting new goals. It also helps to keep people around me who are willing to do that for me as well.

This affects me the most at work when I allow others to make me feel like what I'm doing isn't good enough. I am never entirely sure if others see me as good enough, no matter what they say. This sometimes makes me believe that others might brush off a hard-earned accomplishment of mine as simply luck, causing me to feel stressed. I have fallen victim to workplace bullying, where another teacher felt it was their duty to point out every little mistake I made when I first started teaching. Looking back, that was entirely because I allowed it to happen. I have developed a stronger mind and soul since taking more control of my story and being more in tune with what my strengths and weaknesses are.

Finally, I have a difficult time working with adults who have personalities that are not reliable. If I don't know what kind of reactions or personality traits I'm going to get every time I talk to them, I start to struggle with that person. For good reason, I like predictability and need to trust someone's actions when I work with them. If they are not that way, I struggle with how to react because they are more difficult to read, which is what I use to adjust myself to another person. In working with this kind of person, I not only have a hard time with it, but it actually activates my anxiety. When I find that I am working with a person who is not predictable, I will begin to limit my interactions with them as much as I can.

I have learned that there are times when I need to do what is right for me in order to keep me mentally healthy and recognizing when someone is not good for me is one way that I can do this. But the most important part I've learned from living with depression and anxiety is recognizing that I know it's happening and dealing with it head-on. Being cognizant of my feelings and perceptions is one way for me to battle my inner emotions and determine if they are justified or not.

## My Lessons

It's important to understand that even though I have a sad story, I am not sad about my childhood. I have worked very hard to forgive the people in my life who have had their own struggles that seemed so insurmountable to them that they couldn't love me in the right way. I had to learn to forgive people who have no intention of saying they're sorry.

While my experiences have made me a better person, where they have supported me most is when I became an educator. Honestly, I did not see that coming. It was only after working with kids and figuring out where I belonged that I was able to fully engage the strengths that I had developed as a result of my past. As I've been able to develop those skills further and use them to become the educator I am, I am thankful to have been given the wherewithal to use my superpowers for good instead of evil. I am a stronger person because of my adversity, and my adversity has absolutely sculpted me into the person who was meant to work in education.

For example, I am tenacious and relentless. While some people might look at my mother and I and our different paths, personalities, and choices, I actually do have some of her traits; I just have been given the tools to channel my energies differently. For example, my mother was extremely obsessive. She often collected things. At one time, we had a zoo of strange animals. Foxes, a monkey, pot-bellied pigs, raccoons...and she would spend hours on the computer looking for more. When she latched onto something, it was with complete abandon. Everything else would be ignored until she got her fill with whatever she had her sights set on. In many ways, I can be the same way, but I channel my energy into my work and my passions. This is not only more socially acceptable but has made me successful when I know something is best for students or teachers, and I fully believe that it should happen for them. All you need to tell me is that I can't do something to watch me work until I'm happy with what I've achieved.

I am extraordinarily empathetic. We are all a compilation of our experiences and how we have reacted to their outcomes. Some of our strengths are so embedded in us, so ingrained that it's difficult to separate what we use professionally from who we are as a human. I can be empathetic almost to the point of paralysis sometimes. It doesn't matter the trauma or situation, whether it's at work or at home, I genuinely hurt when other people hurt; I can sense when they are questioning their own worth, and I can feel people's emotions. This level of empathy is difficult to describe because it is so complete.

As a teacher, I could detect better than most what my kids were feeling and felt more in tune with their emotional needs. I worked really hard to make our classroom more like a family because I knew that some kids didn't have that family feeling at home, and every kid deserves to know what that feels like. As a leader, empathy helps me discover where people are uncomfortable and the support they need to move forward. Ignoring fear does nothing to help learning. The fear needs to be recognized and dealt with, so using empathy to determine other's needs significantly increases the chance that I will be able to help them in the way that they need versus the way I want. It definitely helps me be more learner-centered, whether those learners are five or fifty.

I am more perceptive than most. As a child, I learned to be hypervigilant as I walked into a room or came home from school because I needed to be able to read what was going on and adjust my actions accordingly. I learned how to find differences in people's facial expressions and tone, and if they meant that I would be okay to relax or not. I knew when to ask questions and when to be quiet. I learned how to tell the difference between what someone said and their nonverbal cues. I learned what sarcasm meant and how it could be used to make someone feel terrible about themselves.

This enhanced perception has followed me into my adult life and has made me acutely aware of what is going on around me whenever I walk into a new situation. I am constantly surveying a room and reading the people. I notice their little eccentricities, even when they don't realize it. I detect how their vocal tone raises or lowers when their feelings about a topic changes. I recognize things in people that others usually miss, and this is another superpower.

In the classroom, being perceptive allowed me to take a quick dipstick of the overall feeling of my students when the day began, as well as pick up on their individual quirkiness that I knew would drive their day. This worked especially well for two categories of kids: the ones who struggled with their emotions and the ones who were afraid of being at home. In working with adults, my perceptiveness allows me to connect on a deeper level because I am able to adjust my communication to the person I'm working with. My ability to be flexible, adjust, and attend to the things that most people wouldn't pick up, creates a connection that is both deep and quick. It makes me sensitive to their needs and subtle changes, and all these strengths in tandem allow me to both teach and lead in the best way I can for individuals.

The absolute best superpower that I have retained from my experiences is the value that I place on the positive relationships in my life. I've learned that family isn't always related by blood but rather, they are the people who accept your quirks and weirdness, and I do the same for them. People often tell me that they "feel a connection" to me, and they probably do, because it's often there. I also believe that people who have come through adversity carry a certain vibe - like no matter how invisible their scars are, other people with similar scars are drawn to them like a magnet. Trauma changes a person and generally can act as a beacon for other people needing support. So that connectedness that people feel, I credit my story for that.

Bad things happen to people all the time. People choose how they are going to react to their adversity. I have chosen not to be sad, angry, or resentful, but to respond by intense reflection that has shown me who I want to be despite the difficulties, and how I can use the strengths I have gained through my experiences to be a better educator and leader. I am definitely not perfect, but I know that. I am constantly a work in progress. But had I not lived my story, I would not be the person I am today, and I am working every day on being proud of that.

I was recently made aware of a student that I had several years ago speaking about me, asking how she might reach me to say hi, and telling her friends she missed me. This student struggled with negative behaviors in my class, and at first, I was shocked that it was me she was looking for. But when I really thought about it, she connected with me because I treated all my students like I had always wanted my mother to treat me. Sometimes our greatest lessons are taken from people we learn we don't want to emulate. My students were my kids, for better or worse, and they always knew that I cared about them and had their backs. My childhood experiences made this possible. And if I made a difference in the life of even one child, I'd go through every minute of my childhood all over again just to have the superpowers I have today.

# Chapter Three
# Broken Perception

*Ethan Backwell*

> "One small crack does not
> mean you are broken.
> It means you were put to the test
> and didn't fall apart."
> -Linda Poindexter

*Original work by Ethan Backwell*

*Ethan Backwell is an elementary school teacher in Canada. Originally from Australia, where he completed the majority of his education, he moved across the globe to his wife's home city of Calgary. He is now in his 7th year of teaching and is influenced and inspired by the Reggio Emilia approach to learning and inquiry in the classroom. Ethan is also an aspiring artist who produces commissioned work inspired by the wildlife in his new country of residence.*

I grew up by the coast in Southern Australia in a home with two incredibly loving and well-educated secondary teachers. My two inspirational brothers, who through both genetics and hard work, developed the skills to succeed in areas that are naturally respected as the "real" academic subjects. It was pretty clear from an early age that my literacy skills and academics did not match the likes of the rest of my family.

When reflecting on my earliest memories of school, I remember being one of those kids who would cover the words that I had written with my other hand so that no one else could see the embarrassing chicken scratch and inconsistent letter formation. I would like to take comfort in thinking that the reason for such illegible writing was a result of my Montessori kindergarten teacher. At a very young age, she convinced me to swap from using my naturally selected left hand to write and forced me to use my right.

I still have a little chuckle whenever I think about the Montessori pedagogy; it is believed that children are at liberty to choose and act freely within an environment. But at the end of the day, this is a flimsy bit of blame that may very well have had little to no impact on how I would struggle in the future years.

I had an educational psychology assessment conducted on me when I was nine years old to identify where my challenges were. As well as legibility and spelling hurdles, it was found that I also had average decoding and tracking abilities when it came to reading. This dramatically impacted my ability to transfer information from the board or textbook to my notebook.

I would forever lose my place and what others could do effortlessly would take me a considerably long time.

Handwriting and printing were among the numerous literacy challenges that seemed to burden my education. My spelling was and continues to be my kryptonite as well as a lack of confidence in my general knowledge of grammar and punctuation.

My doubts and negative perception of my literacy skills were brought to my attention by being moved to an English support class during high school. It was one of those experiences where you look around at the other individuals and get a quick realization that you have been grouped with "those" struggling kids. Then you sink lower in your chair when you come to terms that you actually belong there.

I remember one of my teachers berating me in front of the class and demanding, "take pride in the name you have been given and print it legibly!" On another occasion, my mother recalled me coming home and being incredibly upset and humiliated because there had been a teacher who was on a prep who walked down an aisle in my class, picked up my work, held it up to the class and said, "I didn't know you were studying hieroglyphics."

My time in high school didn't only bring my literacy challenges to the forefront, but it left a permanent impact on my mental health and negatively impacted my self-esteem. Kids are cruel creatures, and I sure felt my share of this cruelty during those six years. After only a few weeks at my first high school, I soon felt ostracized by the cliquish and tight-knit social dynamics of the coastal crew. I was from a small hamlet a few surf towns away and couldn't seem to break into the scene.

After attending the orientation camp at the start of the school year, I was excluded from a group of guys who I thought were my friends. My mother recalls picking me up after my time away, and I broke down stating that, "I didn't make any new friends and the ones that I thought I had don't like me anymore." My parents decided that I would move schools and attempt to reconnect with some old friends from my primary school.

This second school was located in the nearest city, a bus ride away. I was not put into a homeroom with my old friends; instead, I was placed in a classroom that had already been established, and a clear pecking order was present. It turns out that there was not much flexibility, as the administration team at this school made room for me that was not technically there. Thanks to the extended teacher network, my mother was able to call in a favor from a friend. As a result of my late start to the school, I entered the mix pretty low on that pecking order and remained there for quite some time.

If you saw the beard on my face and the hair on my body, it is hard to believe that in my first year at school I had yet to develop some of the hair that my fellow peers displayed. As a result, I was bullied and accused of shaving my legs. I remember one of the alpha males in my class putting his leg across a walkway during a class and not letting anyone pass unless they said aloud, "Ethan shaves his legs." At the end of the day, I would board the bus where the older boys had given me the nickname, "Effan Gay Bastard." I would go to bed hoping that the next day would be brighter.

An awkward interaction with a girl during one of my early sexual experiences resulted in intimate rumors widely spread around the school. I was locked in a room with another girl at a small house party. The other partygoers thought it would be fun to hold the door shut until something happened between the two of us. This eventuated in embarrassing nicknames, signs being held up against windows as I walked by classrooms and email accounts being created to cyberbully me with secret aliases so my antagonists would not get caught. The effects of this have resulted in ongoing insecurities.

Constant ridicule and bullying tend to wear down the spirit. As a result, my self-loathing and lack of self-worth helped to manifest body image issues. Soon to follow were cycles of starving, binge eating, and periods of excessive exercise. I have memories of dipping the knife into the peanut butter and leaving it in the sink so that my parents would assume that I had eaten breakfast. The hunger pangs were encouraging, and I liked the feeling. I was never successful in throwing up my food. I have a memory of kneeling in front of the toilet attempting to do so, dry heaving, then quickly standing up feeling both shame and shock that I was actually trying to do it.

Around this time, I worked at a grocery store. I recall emptying a box of diet pills into my pockets during one of my shifts so that I could use them when I got home. I hated who I was, and I didn't want to be here anymore.

I am not unique in the fact that I had suicidal thoughts; I never had a plan, but I would daydream about it.

At the time, I worked at a grocery store. I recall emptying a box of diet pills into my pockets during one of my shifts so that I could use them when I got home. I hated who I was, and I didn't want to be here anymore. I am not unique in the fact that I had suicidal thoughts; I never had a plan, but I would daydream about it.

So, as I approached my final years of school, like every student, it was time for me to pick my future by homing in on my career path and the courses that would get me there. I can't actually remember why I chose to be a teacher. I joke about initially wanting to be a primary school teacher for the holidays, and that the majority of the work was going to involve finger painting. To be honest, I think my mum and maybe someone else in my life may have suggested it. But when I really think about it, I do believe that I wanted to return to the classroom to try to make school a positive place for children who felt otherwise. I knew the effects of low self-esteem in school both in the classroom and outside of it. Perhaps I could try to change that for others. And so, I set my sights on teaching.

Understandably, to be accepted into the teaching course at university I needed to have a minimum score in my English year 12 marks. This terrified me. Were the barriers in my literacy skills going to hamper this future career before it even got started? Thanks to the support from my parents and having many tutoring sessions with a close family friend, I was able to successfully reach and in fact score beyond the minimum results required. My brothers' overall year 12 scores were 95 and 98 respectively. I will always remember how proud my parents, mum, in particular, were when I scored my 75. As a result, I applied for and was accepted into the Bachelor of Education Elementary Teaching program.

In total contrast, University was an incredible experience for me. After taking a gap year to work and travel, I started my 4-year course at a university close to home. Here I met an incredibly caring and supporting group of friends who knew nothing of my backstory and saw me for who I really was. In my third year, I participated in the exchange program and spent a semester in Canada at UVIC (University of Victoria Canada). If I could relive a particular time in my life on repeat, it would be those six months spent in Victoria, British Columbia.

Not only was I able to continue to come out of my shell and be accepted - even celebrated for who I was, but I was incredibly fortunate enough to meet a breathtaking girl who would later become my wife and the mother of our child. I consistently received solid marks for my assignments and always spent time with my mother to edit my work for grammatical errors and spelling issues. I can't recall doing anything different to receive such positive results; perhaps it was simply a shift in perspective and a new, more mature environment. At the end of the four years of my confidence-boosting and positive university life, I graduated with distinction and was now ready to step into the classroom, hopeful of making a difference for some little people.

As a student, school was not a very positive place for me. Unfortunately, too many negative situations have tarnished my view of this time of my life. As a teacher, I soon realized that not only did I have to power to make school a positive and supportive environment, I had a responsibility and duty to do so.

I am currently in my seventh year of teaching. This year I am teaching an incredible group of grades 1 and 2 students in Canada. I moved here with my wife, returning to her hometown 4 years ago. The students' self-value, respect, and care for each other is incredibly important to me and is a constant focus. I want my students to walk out of the classroom at the end of the day feeling safe, proud, and with a strong sense of belonging. I frequently acknowledge their academic and personal growth and highlight their achievements to their peers.

I am a pretty emotional guy, both in the positive and negative forms. I have trouble congratulating and praising students to their face or sharing good news stories with their parents without a tear forming in my eye. When I recently spoke to my wife about this reaction, she put it simply. Here I am giving to my students what I craved but rarely received myself in the classroom. I was giving positive feedback about their academic and personal achievements. I feel confident in the connections that I can make with my students and their families because I truly care for each and every one of them. All I can hope for is that they feel confident about who they are and embrace their unique skills and interests.

My literacy skills didn't magically improve. I still have the same challenges as I did when I was going through school. The beauty of my situation is that I can use my areas of need to model for my students. I am vulnerable in front of them and don't shy away or attempt to hide my struggle. I express the pride I have in many areas of my life where I feel confident in my abilities.

On the flip side, I share with my students the areas that I lack confidence in, demonstrating and scaffolding strategies that I use each day to overcome my barriers. I get feedback from my developed spellers when I am unsure about the look of a word that I have written. Can you imagine having your teacher ask you in first or second grade for your advice on a spelling word? It has become the norm in my classroom. They are respectful and kind when they notice an error in my work, and it offers them some great experience with revising and self-correcting strategies. I have the fortune of learning or re-learning spelling patterns alongside the kids, and the discovery and wonder are real.

Thankfully, there has been a constant shift towards using technology in our day-to-day lives, and I have the support of word processing programs and spell checks. I still send my school reports to my mum back in Australia twice a year. We have an ongoing partnership where she identifies grammatical errors, so it is less of a burden on my partner teachers to proofread. It is a bit of a tradition now, and even if my parents are gallivanting around Australia in their slide-on camper, mum will stop into McDonald's stores to access their Wi-Fi and revise my work.

I still find myself getting embarrassed or frustrated when I am typing on the Smartboard for my colleagues to see, and I always opt for a digital form over a handwritten one to avoid any unneeded awkwardness. My fellow teachers are understanding and patient; it is really just me that it affects.

I recently had my parents send me a copy of the assessment that I had when I was in grade four. This was a pretty amazing experience as a teacher and as an adult, to read through the findings of the younger me as a student. The astonishing thing is that out of all 13 areas that were assessed, only 2 were average. The rest were high average, superior and very superior, including scores in the 98th and 99th percentile. Somewhere along the line, I managed to isolate the perception of myself as a learner on the two lower areas rather than the eleven areas that were strong and positive.

As for the baggage that I have carried from my school experiences both academically and socially, I am currently facing these past events with professional and spiritual support with the hope of being able to put them behind me while using them for growth and empowerment. I am aware of the impact that they have on my relationship with my beautiful wife and others in my life. I am comforted knowing that we will both continue to support each other as we positively transform.

*You don't have a right to the cards*
*you believe*
*you should have been dealt.*
*You have an obligation to play the hell*
*out of the ones you're holding.*

Cheryl Strayed
Tiny Beautiful Things:
Advice on Love and Life from Dear Sugar

# Chapter Four

# Victim to Advocate: One Teacher's Story

*Jennifer Johnson*

> "We are all broken, that's how the light gets in."
> -Ernest Hemingway

*Jennifer Johnson worked in Regional Day School Programs for the Deaf as an interpreter, teacher of the deaf, and instructional specialist for almost a decade. She is currently pursuing her doctorate in special education at the University of North Texas where she focuses on research related to child maltreatment prevention in populations with communicative disorders and deafness. Jennifer has worked at Texas Woman's University in a variety of roles since January of 2017. Jennifer welcomes questions and comments about this chapter at jenniferlowejohnson@gmail.com.*

When I entered 3rd grade, I was a pretty happy kid. I loved to play the piano and sing in children's choir. At home, I would make forts with my brother using the kitchen chairs and blankets. One of our favorite games was "lava." Every kid has played that, right? It's where the floor is lava, and you have to jump between pieces of furniture to keep from being destroyed. Classic! I adored going to school and spent a fair amount of time using the extra worksheets my 2nd-grade teacher had given me to play school. The beginning of 3rd grade is the last time I remember being happy-go-lucky like a kid should be.

During that school year, I was sexually abused by an extended family member. I can still remember the details of the room where it took place, and the smells stick with me to this day. My parents had no idea. No one had any idea. Except me. And him. We knew. Starting at the time of the abuse, I had nightmares all the time and frequent vomiting at night. I even remember saying to my mom one night, "I just wanna die."

I didn't know what was happening to me. I just knew I didn't like it and I wasn't allowed to tell. My parents took me to the doctor due to the vomiting, and the doctor concluded there was nothing wrong with me and I was a hypochondriac. Yep. That's right. A hypochondriac. So, I made the meaning of what happened to me; I decided it was normal and I was just a baby for being affected by it.

When I look back on my childhood after the abuse, there's a distinct dark cloud that hangs over it, even in my good memories. I realize now that I was experiencing childhood depression. When you're depressed, even the mountaintop highs feel like little more than small hills, and I think that's why I became such a hard-core overachiever even in areas that I wasn't interested in. I needed more and more mini highs to maintain motivation and energy to function.

I told my parents when I was in fourth grade that I wanted to teach "deaf kids," but it really didn't seem like a very highly respected job as I got older. I don't know when that belief developed or what societal factors led me to conclude that, but teaching didn't seem like something that got anyone very much recognition. Since I was dependent on achievement for those mini highs to get me through, I started looking at other career options. I never could fully break from the dream of teaching "deaf kids" though.

Along with the depression and need for achievement, I recognize a shift in how I processed interactions with men and boys. My perception of boys and men, based on the lens of abuse, was that all they really wanted was my body. We could have good conversations and fun, but when it all came down to it, all that positive interaction was just manipulation in my mind.

When I was 14, I met a boy at a football game through a mutual friend. He showed an interest in me, and I was pretty resistant, but he was persistent. Eventually, we became good friends. He broke the perception I had of men and showed a genuine interest in me as a person. I latched on for dear life. I didn't heed the warning signs that the relationship wasn't healthy because I think deep down, I thought there weren't any other guys out there that would like who I was as a person. I had a very impaired opinion of myself that stemmed from the abuse, but also from the anti-intellectual culture of my school. After the first year of college, we got married. I remember having doubts up until right before the wedding ceremony started. I told myself repeatedly in the months leading up to the wedding and up until minutes before it started that it was just cold feet. This relationship was as good as it got, I thought. But that didn't actually turn out to be the case.

My sophomore year of college, I was still avoiding the teaching profession. I was a Communication Sciences & Disorders major and had plans to get my doctorate in audiology. The tide began to turn when I accepted a job as a nanny for five children. When I took the job, I didn't ask a lot of questions. I was young and naive and willing to work for meager wages.

It turned out that three of the five children had disabilities, and I had no experience with that population. I immediately felt like I was in over my head. The middle child was deaf, so the immediate need upon starting the job was that I learn sign language. I signed up at my university for a sign language class and started carrying around the sign language dictionary.

My professor that semester was Chad Smith. He had taught children who are deaf/hard of hearing for 10 years, and he gave quite a sales pitch for the profession, but I still wasn't buying it. I did need his help though, so I asked him if he could stay after class and give me some tips on how to tutor the child I was nannying who was deaf.

## VICTIM TO ADVOCATE
## JENNIFER JOHNSON

The first night we met, he gave me a simple idea for teaching him the difference in d and b, which was still a struggle for this particular kiddo in 2nd grade. When it was time for homework the next day, I implemented the strategy, and IT WORKED! As I would find more and more of the boy's academic weaknesses, I would ask for advice and Dr. Smith would tutor me in tutoring the boy. Before I knew it, I was hooked. It was a bit like a puzzle...a really complicated puzzle...and I liked it! The next semester I changed my major to Education of the Deaf and never looked back.

When I finally got through my Bachelors and Masters degrees and began student teaching, I had no idea the Pandora's Box that was about to be opened. I student taught at a residential school for children who are deaf/hard of hearing, so I taught during the day and stayed in the dorms on campus at night. My first experience with child maltreatment as a teacher was when a 4th grader in my class came to school with a hickey on her neck, recounting that she and her brother were playing a game.

I remember that evening sitting in my dorm in shock, realizing that it wasn't just me. I found navigating that experience to be a little too close to home given my childhood experiences. I experienced intense anger that this was still going on in the world as if it would've ended with me, but for purposes of self-preservation, I stuffed it all away in the recesses of my mind shortly after it happened. However, I would occasionally have this nagging feeling pop up that I couldn't shake. I felt like I needed to do something about child abuse, surely it didn't have to be this way...but I felt powerless, especially since I still struggled with my own.

Even though I tried my best to stuff away my realizations from student teaching, my first year of teaching would throw the doors right off the jam-packed emotional closet I had stuffed full of my trauma. I will never forget September 18 during my first year of teaching. I sat at my desk at 7:55 am, knowing students would be walking in the door at 8:00 am, on the verge of a panic attack. I felt like I couldn't tolerate being in the presence of my students for one more second and I didn't know why.

That morning, I Googled counselors in the area and made an appointment for that afternoon. It didn't take long in counseling to realize that my anxiety surrounded the realization that eight years old is really young. I always had this idea in my head that when I was abused, I was old enough to know better...that somehow, I was responsible for not saying no or fighting back or not telling anyone. What I realized that semester was that I was a baby. I was a little, innocent kiddo who had no idea what was happening and there's no way I could've been expected to know or intervene in my situation. A long journey of healing began when I finally realized I wasn't alone or responsible for what had happened to me.

While I was navigating healing from the abuse I had experienced, I was also battling chronic illness. I had pretty significant health issues my entire adolescence and into my early 20s. For most of our marriage, I had been sick, and it all came to a head the week before school started my second year of teaching. The Monday before school started I had surgery and that Friday my husband left town to visit his parents. He came back on Sunday and told me he wanted a divorce.

He gave a multitude of reasons over the course of the divorce, but the one that resonated with me the most was that he was tired of being married to a sick person. I couldn't afford to maintain the house on a teacher's salary, so I moved out. For the next two months, I was in and out of the ER on a weekly basis with further issues.

In October that year, about two months after he asked for a divorce, I had a hysterectomy. He didn't show. I remember as I was wheeled into my room after surgery asking my mom for him. I remember her saying, "He's not here, honey." I remember being confused and then realizing "wait.... we aren't together anymore, are we?" He did show up to visit the second day I was in the hospital, but I think that was the moment I realized we were "never, ever, ever, getting back together" ...in the words of Taylor Swift.

After recovering physically from the hysterectomy, I just could not pull myself together emotionally. Abuse. Divorce. Infertility. It was all too much. Before Christmas in 2010 I entered a partial hospitalization outpatient program for treatment of depression and anxiety. At the time they told me the average stay was three weeks. I was there five. I left the clinic with major improvement, but there was so much farther to go to truly experience peace again.

For the next eight years of my life in public schools, I struggled immensely. I went to counseling every week for eight years and still go. I was absent at least my maximum number of allowable days and was partially hospitalized a second time for depression. There were many years where I just didn't know if I could continue being a teacher. However, I found my encouragement and my lifeline in the children I worked with every day. There is one particular child that has had a significant impact on me personally and professionally, and I would like to spend some time telling you about him and his story.

In August of 2011, I took a new job in a new district far away from where I lived when I was married. I wanted a fresh start, and I was excited to see what the year would bring with my new classroom of 3rd-grade kiddos. That year I had a child in my class I will call John.

John had a profound hearing loss and received little benefit from hearing aids. His language functioned between 18 months and 24 months old. His family didn't speak English, and he didn't speak Spanish. They didn't know sign language, and he knew very basic sign language. Communication was a struggle both at home and school, but it was a profound struggle at home. After I started the job, one of the teachers told me that no one wanted to teach John, so they gave his class to the new teacher...that was me.

John had significantly below average social skills and could not read or write. John often smelled like he hadn't bathed in days and he hoarded food frequently enough that I suspected there wasn't much food at home on a regular basis. The school had expressed concerns for years to Child Protective Services, but nothing ever seemed to come of it. On one instance, the school had conducted a home visit and observed a younger child urinating in the corner of the living room, like that was typical behavior. Life was hellish for this kid. That was abundantly clear.

One morning when the bell rang, the kids shuffled into the room, and there was quite a bit more activity than normal. Typically, the kids were tired from riding the bus for so long so they would lay their heads down on their desks until it was time to start. Today was markedly different. They were like busy bees, and all the commotion was centered around John. When I looked up, I immediately noticed that he had severe cuts on his face. He was upset that everyone was pointing at them and asking questions. I knew he could escalate quickly to putting his hands on kids to communicate his displeasure, so I intervened and asked him to come to my desk.

Using the limited language John had in his repertoire along with some pantomime and gestures, he told me that his dad had become angry, pushed him and that he had fallen through the window. First, I was shocked. Then I was angry. Eventually, I was sad. I reported to Child Protective Services what he had told me as I was required to do by law.

When CPS came to interview him, he was unable to communicate in a way that the caseworker and interpreter understood. To my knowledge, nothing ever came of it. That year there was incident after incident that led me to believe the home was an abusive and neglectful environment. For example, later in the year John tried to strangle me with my scarf and grabbed me underneath my skirt, both of which he thought were funny. He gave many descriptions throughout the year of bugs and rats in his home and was constantly covered in bites.

Over the years there was a pattern with this family and CPS. Occasionally, something would happen with a sibling and his mother would be told she had to leave the dad or CPS would take the kids. Every year or so she fled the state and then returned to live with dad again once the case was closed. I have spent many sleepless nights worrying about this kid and what could change his world. He hasn't been my student in 6 years, and I still think about him frequently. He's the inspiration for the work I currently do.

It became clear to me after observing John's life and many other similar lives that I could not change what was happening to my students from where I was in public education. I didn't want to continue to file reports year after year. I wanted to prevent the reports. I didn't know how to do that, but I had to take a risk in order to learn. I began to contemplate going back to school to get my Ph.D. to give me the credentials to become an influential part of public policy making and primary prevention research. I landed at the University of North Texas majoring in Special Education with a concentration in Emotional/Behavioral Disorders.

Shortly into my Ph.D. program, I attended a conference: The Association of College Educators – Deaf and Hard of Hearing, in New York. There I met a man by the name of Harold Johnson, Ph.D. who was heading up a Child Maltreatment Work Group that would focus on preventing the maltreatment of children who have communicative disabilities. I remember sitting in disbelief and thinking, "This is it! This is what I've been looking for! This is my pathway to living fully and wholeheartedly in the direction of my dreams."

This Work Group was a grassroots effort to have protective factors included as part of Individual Education Plans for students with communicative disabilities. Translation: We wanted teachers planning abuse prevention into every child's plan who struggles with communication. A three-fold plan was developed to address the issue: 1) Awareness & Understanding, 2) Recognition & Reporting, and 3) Prevention & Responding. A "Safety Letter" with information and resources for educators was published for the first time in September of 2017. This is a big step towards the further creation of public policy in the area of prevention of the maltreatment of children with disabilities.

As I do research in child maltreatment, I think of John often. He is in high school now. Unfortunately, his life situation hasn't gotten better, and over the past couple of years, my biggest fear has been that he would end up in prison. Because of my fear, I started researching the population of people who are deaf/hard of hearing in prison and found some startling case studies. It turned out in these case studies that people who were in the justice system and were DHH were largely illiterate, had low levels of functional language, and had endured significant abuse as a child. This is exactly my former student's experience. When I made that connection, my superpower began to become more fine-tuned.

I am now in a period of my career where I am experiencing empathy for a group of people who are abusers themselves. In the depths of my depression and in my desires for revenge, I have wished many an abuser dead. (That's the PG version). Now I find myself feeling significant empathy for this group of prisoners, who in case the world forgot, were once eight-year-old children who had no idea what was happening to them either.

I hope that the research I'm embarking on now will help teachers identify abuse more effectively, to intervene quicker, and to break the cycle of abuse which has led many people to prison, especially those with disabilities. The most significant tragedy of my life has somehow become one of my biggest strengths. And that, my friends, is all I can hope for in this life. I get out of bed every morning deeply committed to teaching, research, and child abuse prevention because 20 years ago a wounded man took out his woundedness on me. I've always thought until recently that I would go back and change it if I could, but I've realized lately that the trauma I experienced has been the impetus for greatness in my life, both personally and professionally. I wouldn't change a thing.

As for my personal recovery…I still struggle. However, the struggle is not quite as visceral as it used to be, nor does it feel as daunting and powerful. I'm more emotionally stable than I've ever been. I don't get sad inside every time I see a baby that I'll never have biologically. And I'm remarried to possibly the most incredible man who has helped me learn that I don't have to be perfect to be loveable.

I've developed strategies to stay grounded in triggering moments and most importantly, I've found ways to reroute the negative thought patterns I developed because of the abuse. (Mindfulness and meditation have been lifesavers.) However, the most meaningful and effective strategy has been, and continues to be, finding meaningful ways to use what I went through as a catalyst for future good in the world.

For anyone who has been abused…I pray that you would find deep, meaningful ways to find purpose in your survival, that you would wake up every day knowing that you have the potential to make a difference in the life of a child through every minor interaction, and that you would find hope in my story that helps you to continue to fight to survive yours.

# Chapter Five
# The Power Within

*Dene E. Gainey*

> *"Be fearless in the pursuit of what sets your soul on fire."*
> -Anonymous

*Dene Gainey is a passionate and inspired educator of 12 years, an author, and a singer. Building bridges and being an example for students is an extreme passion as well as helping them to C.L.I.M.B.E. through cultivation, leadership, inspiration, motivation (mentoring), building and empowerment. Other passions include diversity & community, the student-driven classroom and mentoring. He has recently published his first solo book titled "The 'Y' in You," which speaks of a journey and the importance and realization of the "why" in you. He may be reached via his site at www.denegainey.com or on Twitter at @dene_gainey.*

## Introduction

When I think about the word adversity, I think about the challenges or obstacles that one faces in life that have the power to limit, take, subtract, or minimize. I can't tell you that I love adversity, but one thing I have come to realize is that adversity does come with inherent power to find yourself in the middle of it, and to be better because of it.

## Part One: Rejected!

My story of adversity is twofold and literally begins with rejection. Growing up, I was that student who performed admirably in school and never truly ran into any academic or behavioral challenges that would prevent me from having success. Even as a college student, I was always driven to be and to do. I involved myself in a myriad of activities that I thought would help me as well as the group or organization I joined. I've always had the desire to "help" others, genuinely so. I can recall the number of years and hours spent going back to my first-grade teacher's classroom to help her with classroom tasks. Perhaps that was because she accepted me. She encouraged me. She built me up. She was a positive light which could not be hidden.

I used to always wonder why I'd see other people with "friends" and felt like I didn't have any for a huge part of my life. I would watch the close ties that others had and started to question my relevance and why I was not experiencing the same things. I started to doubt myself to the degree that I backed myself into a corner.

I'd tried to reach out to people to gain friends, but usually, that ended up backfiring on me, being a one-way street or finding people who were not truly sincere. For example, I'd always sought friends that were fun, creative, and perhaps more extroverted than myself. I'd reached out to one individual and tried to keep in touch as much as possible only to be met with feeling like I was being a bother. This was because I seemed to be the one who was always trying to make contact. It was not a mutual situation. It quickly became a drain and made me question myself as if to validate or affirm that I was okay, I wasn't crazy - or was I expecting too much?

Somehow by nature, I give, and I love doing that. I feel like it's who I am. Nevertheless, constantly giving does have an impact on you when you never "get back." This furthered the negative thought process in my mind, and I isolated myself. There were times that I'd become emotional too because I said to myself, *"I am a good person, positive, genuine, giving...why is it that I don't have friends, why am I feeling like this?"* That was a question that filled my thoughts constantly and was not easily or quickly answered.

## Part Two: What I Could Not Change

I am proud to be an African-American male educator in the elementary area. That makes me a minority twice over. I would have never envisioned that this would create adversity for me. Students need role models, examples, mentors...all of which I strive to be on a daily basis, from my very high expectations of all students, to the compassion I feel when I know a child's heart, and I am fully connected.

I would have never thought that I'd experience prejudice while seeking to educate the generations. I never thought the day would come that the color of my skin would be permission for parents and students to challenge me (on multiple occasions) to the degree that they would go to my boss and seek to tear down, bring division, and who knows what else.

Now let me be clear, it was not simply the color of my skin that was in operation here. Add in my zeal and my motivation to change the world to the mix, and that I bring multiple experiences to the classroom to have students gain a well-rounded experience. I am creative by nature, having had much experience in the arts (writing, singing, acting, playing instruments). I am also a veteran of the US Air Force. Generally, I am a learner, and I learn with students, further motivating them to immerse themselves in learning. Also, I like making learning fun. All things considered, when kids go home they talk about me - hopefully all good things.

I am not different than any other teacher with regards to my humanity. However, I can't even begin to tell you the level of frustration, turmoil, disheartenment, and sadness I have experienced over the 12 years that I have been a classroom teacher. Negativity, judgment, and the "wrong thing" seem to not be far away when trying to do the right thing. The song that comes to mind that I must constantly remind myself of is the old adage that comes to mind, *"What doesn't kill you makes you stronger."* It's true, and sometimes you have to force yourself to see it that way.

Suffice to say that parents have gone to my boss, totally skipping over me, to complain about what they felt was "wrong" with my teaching practices. Complaints ranged from my "being in school to earn a Ph.D. being a limiting factor in [my] ability to perform [my] duties effectively" to "[their] kid going home and speaking of [me] constantly," as if something must have been wrong that their child talked so much about me. The latter of the two experiences was so heartbreaking because I'd connected with the student, perhaps on a level that the mother didn't, and it seemed to be perceived as a threat.

Back in 2006, I had a phenomenal group of fifth-grade students. I was also in charge of the Student Council, which again included many dedicated and motivated fifth graders who were excited to learn, grow, and excel in whatever task was placed in front of them. It is always a goal to connect with my students. A few of these connections were very strong, as I always sought to get to know their parents also and ensure their parents knew me.

At this point, you might say I was the teacher who everyone knew - not only because I was a black male (rare) in elementary education, but because I was creative, a singer, and an actor. (Incidentally, all of my homeroom students came to see me perform in Seussical the Musical the year after this incident occurred.) We developed a bond through interactions we had in class as well as extra-curricular activities. I try to be funny and more importantly "fun," to engage kids and give them a space where they are free to be themselves and to learn in a least-restrictive environment.

This particular parent, as she put it, would always "hear stories" about me when the student came home. Totally out of my control, but it was me being the engaging, fun, and innovative teacher I love to be. This quickly escalated to, "Something must be wrong here, so let me call the principal and investigate." Needless to say, I felt disrespected and looked over, and I could not figure out why the parent would not come to me rather than going to my boss at the time. It honestly hurt my feelings that the parent seemed to not have confidence enough in me to allow me to deal with the situation, which actually was not a situation at all, as it turned out.

Thus, I had to schedule a meeting. At this point, to discourage further conflict, I invited my boss, the grade-level chair, and the parent. I'd also made an officer friend aware of my situation, and she made herself available for the meeting as well.

Long story short, the mom realized that she'd been in the wrong and I gained strength from being able to demonstrate that. It still took a toll on my emotions, my mentality, and truthfully made me restructure how certain things were done to a degree, to try to alleviate such things from happening again. This was adversity. This was unbelievable for me. My only desire as an educator is to change the world. That is what it was when I started, and it will continue to be that until the day comes that I hang it up.

## My Superpower

Have I overcome the negative influence of rejection? One thing I realize is that feeling rejected is not fun, but it forced me to push harder in other ways. It reinforced my passion to not give up on what I believe my purpose was to be on this earth. It made me want to excel even more because despite what I felt, I knew in the back of mind that this couldn't be "it" for me. There had to be somewhere else to move forward. There had to be a happy place somewhere. I quickly realized that rejection can aid in moving you into your purpose. Had I been accepted by everyone, I may not have gained so much knowledge through continued learning and advanced degrees. Had I been accepted by those who I thought should accept me (rather than judge me), I may have been in a much worse quandary. Had I not experienced rejection, I may not have had the will or the power within to keep going and moving and doing and acting and being.

For many reasons, I feel like this experience has merit or value on my ability today to have compassion for others who encounter the same types of things. This is not limited to adults but also for my students in the classroom, who for whatever reason, are not accepted by their peers. I become their affirmation because I know that rejection isn't pleasant. Yet I understand that if I am willing to help them see the power in it, they too will understand that it is not all bad but can have positive benefits.

Today, I stand convinced that rejection was not without purpose. There was purpose in all the pain that I experienced that affected me emotionally, mentally, psychologically, and physically. I am not who I was, nor am I what I went through. I have been given the opportunity to be more than my limited perspective would have allowed me to be if I had not been exposed to rejection.

Though rejection does not feel good, it is sometimes the path that leads to acceptance and real friends that care and it's not necessary to convince them to do so. They care. They give. They love. They support. They urge on, just like my first-grade teacher who I will NEVER forget. Making connections are like plugging yourself into a socket or power outlet. It gives you charge and energy to keep pushing forward and "working." Thus, I can rely on those connections during adverse times to re-energize me when life sucks the energy out of me. It's not the number of friends you have but the quality therein. Through those relationships and opportunities to write about my experiences, I can overcome future adversity which I know will come.

## Superpower Produces Super Students

Students need role models; they need people who will accept them, love them, relate to them and simply be there for them. That physiological need is always a priority over the academic need; otherwise, the academic need is not met. I am now an advocate for students. My classroom is a place of peace and comfort where students are eager to come in and just "be." They know I am going to redirect and guide, but they ultimately know that it is because I care. Everything I teach has some aspect of life infused in it. I tell them, "this isn't about your fourth or fifth-grade year, it's about life." Rejection led to acceptance. Discomfort bred comfort. Dislike produced love that is real and unabridged.

What I am is grateful. I can't say that I don't still experience rejection, but what I can say is that I know how to use that rejection as fuel. It has inspired me to reach higher and strive longer and dig deeper for the greater me within myself.

# Chapter Six
# From Adversity to Art

*Darren Conley*

> "I survived because the fire inside me burned brighter than the fires around me."
> -Joshua Graham

*Darren Conley is currently completing his 31st year as an educator. He helps support school districts and community schools in a three-county region in Northern Ohio around the social-emotional needs of students and families. He engages educators to build their capacity to support students with social, emotional, and behavioral challenges. Outside of work, you may find him enjoying time with his family and friends or engaged in activities in Nature's Sanctuary.*

My story begins on a pig farm in the central Ohio town of Marion. There was a particularly heavy snowfall that January day back in 1963 as I first opened my eyes to this big new world. Of course, I don't remember my first thoughts but somehow, that smell; the pungent, earthy, ammonia-laced odor of a pig farm, always makes me feel like I'm home. My family, Mom, Pat, Dad, Keith, and a brother, Tim, eighteen months older than me, found ourselves on that farm for a reason. You see, a judge from Marion County owned that farm and my father had found himself in front of that judge after he was involved in some pretty illegal activity.

After serving some prison time, the judge, who had taken a liking to my father, allowed our family to stay in the farmhouse in return for working his pig farm. My mom tells stories of me crawling in the pen with a mother sow and what a stir I caused when the sow started squealing her disapproval of me being there! It was during my first six months there on the farm that I realized that life could be a pretty tough place to be. I honestly feel that I remember this, but it might be from hearing the story told that I have formed this picture of an event that, among many others, would help shape my life.

My father, Keith, was an alcoholic and drug addict. When he was sober, he could be kind. When he was drunk or high, I never knew what to expect. One evening he had been drinking, and he thought it was time to make sure my brother, Tim, now two years old, would learn to fight. As my mother walked into our living room, Keith was holding me up by the hands, facing Tim, and instructing Tim to hit me. "Hit him in the belly, now the head, harder, now the belly," Keith laughed as he held me there, helpless to protect myself. My mother intervened but knew all too well that she too, had to be cautious or she might become Keith's punching bag. Over the next four years, I would witness that horror many times. The holes in our lath and plaster walls that my mother's head had made as Keith violently smashed her into them was evidence of the madness that routinely found its way into our home.

My family bounced around from place to place until I was about four-years-old. We were kicked off the farm because Keith violated his parole and had to serve more prison time. At about age four, we were living in a duplex home near the county fairgrounds. After another violent night, my mother waited for Keith to leave for his job at a factory everyone called "The Shovel."

When Mom was sure he was gone, she grabbed our bag that she had packed while Keith slept off his high, a bag of Chips-Ahoy cookies, and we began our new journey. Her desperate plan was that we would hitchhike to a relative's house in northern Ohio, about a two-hour drive from Marion. At the ages of five and four, Tim and I really had no idea what was going on, but we were with Mom, and we had cookies, so we were good!

After walking about twelve miles that day, we were spotted by a doctor whom my mother had worked for as an LPN. One look at mom's swollen and bruised face left little doubt in the doctor's mind as to the reason we were on the road that late May day. The doctor drove us to the nearby city of Bucyrus (Byoo-seye'-rus) and gave my mom the change she needed to call my Uncle Joe. A couple hours later, Uncle Joe pulled up and took us to his house in northern Ohio. I remember being so happy about that day because also living at Uncle Joe's house was one of my first heroes, my Mamaw! Mamaw was my mom's and Uncle Joe's mother and she, in my mind, was magical!

Mamaw was also a woman of deep Christian faith. When I was a boy, Keith always kept his sons' hair cut very short. He would set us in a chair and run the clippers next to our scalp and, voila, instant buzz cut. Spotting my short blonde hair were five darker spots that Mamaw always told me was, "The Good Lord's hand, guiding you to someday do great things!" And this is my first superpower; the deeply held belief that I was destined to be great!

At times when I was feeling down and depressed about things, Mamaw would remind me of that handprint and of my destiny. Mamaw had twelve children, two of whom had died as infants, leaving her with five boys and five girls. Mom was the baby of the whole bunch. Mamaw managed to raise those ten children on a coal miner's wage in deep West Virginia. Uncle Joe had years ago left West Virginia to work in the new auto factory in northern Ohio. That's how we ended up there that day in Elyria (E-leer'-ee-a) Ohio, a place I call my hometown.

Although I went to bed safe and happy that night, I woke up and was very confused. As I came down the stairs shaking the sleepies from my head, I noticed a huge rifle leaning against the wall at the bottom of the steps.

When I rounded the corner, I saw Uncle Joe with his brother, Uncle Bob, who had a shotgun leaning against the couch close to where he was sitting.

Guns were not a foreign concept to me, as Keith frequently carried pistols and knives and also frequently left them around our house. This was different because as I remember it, this was the first time I discovered another of my superpowers... reading nonverbal messages that people subconsciously give off, which I would later learn is called hypervigilance. I could just sense that something was really wrong. As I looked at the clothespins holding the curtains together where they met, my mind began to wonder; what could be happening?

It hadn't taken long for Keith to realize that we had left and then to figure out where we were. Late the previous night, Keith called my Uncle Joe and said he was heading to Elyria with a gun and four bullets. Keith said, "The bullets each have a name, Pat, Tim, Darren, and my own." He planned to kill us and then himself. I overheard Mamaw saying to her sons, "Keith's a coward, I don't think he has the guts to show his face around here!" Still, for several days, my uncles (both of whom were World War II veterans) manned their posts to keep us safe. Mamaw was right. Keith never showed, but I recall thinking how strange it was being cooped up like that.

Somehow even after all of this, mom let Keith back into our lives and in short order mom became pregnant again. One evening during the summer of 1969, after mom had her third child, my sister Darlene, Keith became enraged during one of his binges. Tim was thrown across the room and into a wall. Two of his ribs fractured. I was punched in the face with Keith's full fist. I ended up with a fractured cheekbone. Finally, mom had developed the courage to stand up to Keith. She told him that it was over and this time he knew it was time for him to move out.

We moved into a house of our own and Mom got a job at a local factory. Luckily a kind man who lived across the street worked at that same factory, so she rode to work and back home with him. We grew accustomed to getting ourselves ready for school and coming home to do our chores while we waited for mom to get home from work. Tim and I, at nine and seven-years-old, would warm up pot pies for our dinner while we waited for mom to pick Darlene up from the sitter's house. Pot pies in those days were ten for a dollar. That's why we ate them every day for years. To this day, pot pies are like kryptonite to me! The smell, the taste, the way they look, everything about them just turns my stomach!

It was also during this time that some of the trauma-induced behaviors from our days with Keith started to rear their ugly head in my brother. I suppose it was difficult to have his father, the one who was created to show Tim how to succeed in the world, teach him to abuse his little brother and then expect him to not continue to do it. With Mom so busy with work and then too tired when she came home to really be present with us, Tim had lots of opportunities to continue his abuse.

It was during this time that I first remember using my most important superpower. This superpower helps me more than any of the others, and it helps ME more than it helps others; the superpower of forgiveness. Though I often had bruises all over me from my brother, I knew deep down inside that he loved me. I also knew deep down inside that he couldn't help himself. He needed someone to connect with, to guide him, to love him through this time. Unfortunately for Tim, there was no one he would allow in, no one he would permit to help him. So, at the age of seven, I had a choice: I could hate, or I could forgive.

Hate would seem to be the easier option. Hate doesn't take a lot of energy, I thought. But hate, and the anger and violence that accompany it, is what I had experienced. At such a tender age, somehow, I managed to choose to forgive. I attribute the formation of this superpower to my Sunday mornings with Mamaw. I would sit next to her in that hard, wooden pew at the Elyria Church of God. The smell of cedar filled the air, and everyone was dressed in their Sunday best!

I remember so vividly hearing Mamaw pray. She would have conversations with God about everything! She would sing with all of her energy and raise her hand in the air. I always wondered why the pastor never answered anyone's questions. As I looked around, all the grownups were raising their hands. In my world that meant they had a question. But no one ever asked a question, and no one was ever called on.

Even with her job though, Mom couldn't make ends meet for our growing family. She went to the welfare office and applied for food stamps. In my mind, food stamps were amazing! The nice ladies at the welfare office gave us this strange looking money that we tore out of books when we bought groceries. Sometimes we used them at a neighborhood store that was only about five blocks from our house. I realized the food stamps weren't so amazing one day when my mom asked me to walk to the store to get some bread and milk. I found the cheap brands, the only brands we ever bought, and got in line behind an older couple.

When it was my turn, I lifted the bread and milk up onto the counter and greeted Mr. Palas, the store owner. He rang me up, and I reached into my pocket and handed the food stamps up to him. The older lady in front of me took note of what I was doing and gave me a look that conveyed both her pity and disgust at the transaction. That picture of the couple standing there, slightly shaking their heads before pushing their cart out to their car has never left my mind. It was a slow walk home that day. I had to keep shifting the bag of groceries from one arm to the other, trying to not crush the bread before I got home.

That day I determined that whatever it took, I would never, ever use food stamps when I was a grown-up. The shame that I felt from a couple that I would never again see was so powerful that it motivated me to start to plan for a future.

Before Christmas that year, Keith found himself back in the custody of the Ohio State Reformatory. The following summer we took a trip to Marion after baseball season to spend time with Keith's mom, Grandma Hazel. We had an amazing time with her.

One day, Grandma Hazel packed Tim and me up in her car, and we all drove to see Keith in prison. We pulled up to the front of a building, the likes of which I could only remember seeing in books about old castles in Europe. The old limestone had been stained by the storms of time, and the sorrow held captive within its walls. As we entered the building through the huge, old wooden doors, we were greeted by similarly huge men in uniforms. There were shoe prints painted on the floor and handprints painted on the walls. One of the huge men told me to put my shoes on the painted shoe prints and put my hands on the handprints on the wall.

As I stepped onto the area as instructed, I noticed how small my little shoes were compared to the prints on the floor. I stretched up as high as I could, but my hands couldn't reach the prints, so the guard told me to just put my hands flat against the cold concrete wall. Once I was in position, the guard gripped my shoulders tightly, ran his hands down the length of my arms and patted my chest, belly, and back. He then grabbed my waist and patted the back pockets of my jeans before sliding his hands down the length of my legs, occasionally squeezing until he touched my ankles. He then asked me to take my shoes off, which I did, even though I knew he would see the holes in my socks.

After putting my shoes back on, Grandma Hazel, Tim and I were taken to the back of the room and told to stop in front of a massive iron gate, painted the same dirty white color as the walls. The guard shouted to another uniformed man behind the desk, and the gate clanged and started opening. We stepped through, only to be greeted by another dirty white gate. As we stood there, the gate behind us slammed shut making a sound so loud that it took my breath away. We must have passed through four or five of those gates before coming to a room that was separated into stalls just like the old pig barn.

At the end of each stall was a window and a phone. Under the window was a metal shelf, painted the same color as everything else in that place. Under the shelf were two metal stools bolted to the floor. Grandma sat us down and told us that Keith would be out in just a minute. As I sat there, I wondered what must he have done to be locked up in such a miserable place? How dangerous was he to have to be kept behind so many gates? I was brought back to reality when I saw a face appear in the window. It looked like Keith, but his face was so thin, and his hair was cut short like mine, a big difference from the last time I had seen him.

Keith picked up the phone on his side of the window, and Grandma picked up our phone. She started to talk to him and almost immediately began to cry. I couldn't hear what Keith was saying, but Grandma just kept crying, and I started getting sad because she was so upset. After a few minutes, she handed Tim the phone. I looked through the window at Keith and tears were now running down his cheeks. They talked for a few minutes and then Tim handed me the phone. I heard Keith's voice for the first time in over a year, but my mind floundered, looking for something to say. What does one say to someone on the phone while looking at them through a window? I closed my eyes, and it seemed to be easier.

I truly don't remember what we talked about, but I do remember Keith telling me to put my hand up against the glass, and to ask Tim to do the same thing. As we stretched our hands out on that cold glass, Keith put the phone on the shelf and put his hands up to ours. Of course, we never really touched but I supposed that was as close as we would be for a couple years. He looked at us with his sad blue eyes apologizing to us and revealing the depth of his anguish, tears streaming down and dripping from his cheeks. I couldn't bring myself to cry because ironically, Keith had always forbidden his boys from crying in his presence. "If you wanna cry, go see your mommy," he always barked at us anytime we dared shed a tear near him.

Grandma took the phone and said she would see him in a few weeks. We waved goodbye to Keith through the glass and watched him walk back toward the guard who was standing near him. Driving away from the prison, I turned, and as the old limestone disappeared behind the rolling green hills, I made another commitment to myself. I would never, ever end up in prison.

With everything that was happening in my life, I began to read books and found that they were a great escape from life. One day as I was looking in our basement for other books to read, I found a dirty white envelope addressed to my mom with the words Lima Correctional Hospital printed in the return address area. Being curious and thinking that this might be a letter from Keith, I pulled the paper out of the already opened envelope.

"Mrs. Conley," the letter started, "We are writing to you to inform you of the results of psychological testing that has been conducted with Inmate Conley. After a thorough battery of assessments, we have concluded that Inmate Conley has been found to be criminally insane." The letter contained a few more paragraphs, but that was all I could read. Criminally insane... what did that mean? Images from Saturday night movies of wild-haired people in straitjackets flooded my brain. My father was criminally insane! What did that make me? What about Tim and Darlene? What does an eleven-year-old boy do when he finds out that his father is criminally insane?

I didn't know what to do, but I knew I didn't want to ask Mom about it. She had put that letter in the basement for a reason, that reason being that I wouldn't see it. I would have loved to ask Mamaw or Uncle Bud about it, but they were not around anymore. So, I did something that would become a pattern for me when I didn't know what to do...nothing. I put the letter back on the shelf and picked up another book. I tried to bury the thoughts of Keith being criminally insane deep in my brain. If I could put it there on a shelf in the basement of my head, no one would know about it. I could leave it there, let it collect dust, and I would never have to look at it again. I took my book and walked back upstairs and sat down on my bed.

In the spring of 1974, Grandma Hazel called and asked if we wanted to come to her house in Marion. "Your dad is coming home, and he's excited to see you, kids," she said, almost pleading for us to come and see him. "And your cousins down here want to see you, too!" Grandma Hazel had moved to a different house in

Marion, and as we carried our bags up the front steps, Keith walked out the front door with a smile beaming from his face. He practically yanked me up off the top step and squeezed me so hard that I could barely breathe! Keith carried me into the house while Tim and Grandma followed us in.

We settled in. Grandma had made one of her specialty dishes - fried chicken with fried potatoes and her homemade corn salsa, for dinner. We enjoyed our first few days there, and Keith stayed with us the whole time. Tim and I slept upstairs in the finished attic bedroom. The ceiling sloped up to a flat spot right in the middle of the room above the queen-sized bed. One day, the four of us spent the day at Aunt Linda's house (Keith's sister) with all of our cousins.

At the end of a fun time, Tim asked if he could stay overnight at Aunt Linda's house. Keith thought that would be a good idea, so Grandma Hazel, Keith, and I headed back to Grandma's house. On the way back, Keith asked if I wanted some ice cream. Knowing I would love that, he pulled into a little store near Grandma's house and came out with two paper bags full of snacks. I could hear bottles clanging together inside the bags, and I thought maybe we were going to make root beer floats!

As we walked into the house, Keith put the bags on the table and walked toward the back porch. I heard him talking to someone in the backyard and could smell pot as it wafted through the screen door. As Grandma took the snacks out of the bags, a disgusted look filled her face as she looked out back, shaking her head. She put the ice cream in the freezer and told me to get ready for my bath.

I slid down into the warm bubbles that Grandma had made for me. I loved letting my arms float on the top of the bathwater as my imagination drifted off to the Navy movies that I loved to watch.

I was shaken back to reality by angry voices downstairs. "I told you there would be no alcohol or drugs in my house, Keith," Grandma shouted, her voice cracking with anger. "Mom, I haven't had a drink in years," Keith barked back at her. "Why do you have to be such a bitch all the time? I just want to relax!" I heard the bottles clank together and then heavy footsteps before hearing that familiar sound of the door slamming.

Grandma came up and looked in on me, telling me to finish up and that we could watch the Dean Martin Show while we ate our ice cream. I put my shorts and T-shirt on and headed down to watch TV with Grandma Hazel. Keith had left, but that really didn't bother me. I loved being with Grandma, and before long, I started to doze off. I went upstairs to the attic bedroom and quickly fell asleep.

As I look back on these events now, it is as if they happened to someone else. As I became an adult, I ended up marrying my high school sweetheart, but not knowing how to have a healthy relationship, that didn't work out. In the two years we were married, we had a little girl named Courtney.

During my first year of college, I took a Psychology 101 class where I learned that many children who were abused often grow up to be abusers. I always had an internal fear that I had the potential for my own "criminal insanity," and having a child scared me to death! This failed marriage, however, caused me to take a step that would change my life. I decided, even against the wishes of my mom and my step-father, John, that talking to a counselor might be what I needed. "Agh," John said, "You don't need to talk to anyone, they just take your money anyway." The pain that I was in and the thoughts I was having of ending my own life, were enough to persuade me to seek help.

I had bounced around from job to job, even joining the Air Force, due to the autoimmune diseases and chronic pain that had started to rack my body, this didn't work out too well, either. I did very well in the Air Force, graduating from a very difficult Tech School with honors. I was asked to stay on at Chanute Air Force Base to teach my specialization, Aircraft Instrument Systems. It was there that I found my love for teaching.

After earning my Associate Degree in Education, I ended up finding my career passion at a place called Edison School, in Elyria. Edison was a separate school for children in grades K-12 who had been identified as having a Severe Behavior Handicap. In those days, Edison was called a "Day Treatment Center." The country was beginning to deinstitutionalize children with social/emotional challenges but held onto the medical model for supporting them. My job there was to assist licensed teachers in supporting those students and to track and keep data on each child's behavior.

I found that I was pretty gifted in working with these "throw-away" kids. My ability to detect the slightest shift in non-verbal cues, to listen, actively listen, and to adapt to my surroundings, allowed me to intervene with and support children through their worst episodes.

I was in my second year at Edison when my marriage fell apart. A friend there, Mary Ellen, gave me the name of a therapist who had really helped her. The man's name was Charlie Startup, and over the next several years he would help me unravel the huge ball of emotional yuck that had been kept there, in the basement of my brain for so long.

It was also during this time that I met another of my colleagues at Edison. She was a beautiful young woman named Ann, who was also going through the breakup of her own marriage. We would talk and help each other through our daily work and life challenges. Although Charlie cautioned me that I shouldn't make any major life decisions during the level of therapy in which I was involved, I couldn't keep myself from falling in love with Ann. She was incredible, and I knew it.

Another major decision I made at that time, was to become a licensed teacher so I could have my own classroom to support the students I had grown to love. Just like everything else in my life, this would not be an easy task. I had to work full time to pay my bills. I also had at least two full years of college courses left to get my teaching license. The nearest school that licensed teachers in this field was Kent State University - about an hour and twenty-minute drive from Edison.

There were two skills that I had developed that allowed me to believe I could achieve my goal: the work ethic that I mentioned earlier and a teacher friend saying, "There is no way you will ever be able to do that!" All my life I had been rising to challenges and outperforming others' expectations of me. My friend telling me I couldn't was all I needed to hear, and I accepted that challenge and took it on with all my energy.

It took four years and lots of miles on my little Ford Festiva but, I did it! I would work all day at Edison, then load up in the Festiva and head down the turnpike to Kent. I could make it there for a 5:00 class and would leave Kent about 10 o'clock at night after sitting through two classes. I would get home and do homework until about 1:00 in the morning, sleep for a few hours and wake up to do it again. I often look back and wonder how I did all that. Survival is the only answer I can come up with. I did what I had to do at that time, with the set of challenges and supports I had. Could I do it again? I like to think that the answer is yes, but I hope to never have to prove that. In November of 1991, I married my best friend, Ann. Now, 26 years later we are very happily married and have three children; Courtney, Jacob, and Bradley. When people ask me about my greatest blessings in life, I see those four smiling faces and am very proud that we are a family. I finally have the peaceful home that I always dreamed of!

The principal at Edison School, Darrel, who would also become one of my best friends, saw my determination and my leadership skills. He encouraged me to join a Principalship Cohort, and that's what I did. As the world entered a new millennium, I received my Master's Degree in Educational Administration from

Bowling Green State University. In the fall of 2001, I found myself as a first-time principal in the historic rural village of Wellington, Ohio. I distinctly remember walking the halls of McCormick Middle School, a Public Works Administration project that was built in 1929, and thinking, "They have enough trust in me to leave me in charge of this whole building!" Choosing to drive the country roads to work many mornings, I was greeted by that "country smell," that reminded me of home. My ability to form deep, meaningful relationships with the educators, parents, and students in my building helped me start my administrative career on a positive note. I would need it because, after about ten school days that fall, America suffered the terror attacks that would change our country forever. Our school building was put on alert because Flight 93, the plane that would eventually be crashed into a field in Shanksville, Pennsylvania, turned around directly over Wellington. I remember manning my post at the back door of our historic school building and releasing children to their parents, watching as they grabbed their children and held them tightly not knowing what tomorrow would bring.

    Leading our school team to improve our academic performance was an achievement of which I was very proud! We set goals, developed action plans, and set about our work with students using strategies that research told us would make a difference. There was a morning after receiving our scores on the updated state assessments that the staff literally danced in the halls, knowing that our work made a difference in these students' lives! The School Report Card came out and right there on the top were the words, "McCormick Middle School, Rating: Excellent." Next to those words, "Principal: Darren K. Conley." It was still very cool to see my name printed next to something that made people happy!

Word travels fast when administrators do well! I was contacted by my friend, Darrel, to ask if I would be interested in coming back to be a principal in Elyria. I did go back and eventually became the principal of Elyria High School, the same school from which I graduated about 27 years earlier. The district needed a person who could keep the peace while moving the 165 staff members and 2,300 students forward as a new high school was built on the same site where the school was currently sitting. Educators might be the only people who would understand this but, I had to tell the teachers at Elyria High that they would no longer be able to park their cars in the spots they had pulled into, some of them, for the past 37 years.

I was skilled at keeping the peace, but I was not skilled at the political aspects of being a large high school principal. With all my abilities to see individual dynamics, I have been told that I am naive when it comes to reading groups of people, especially groups of people who have an agenda of which I am unaware. I am optimistic almost to a fault and choose to believe that people always have good intentions. Though I do not shy away from conflict, I am definitely not at my best when I find myself in it.

In 2008, I received a call from my Aunt Linda telling me that Keith had fallen on icy steps and suffered a severe head injury. I drove with my sister and wife to the Ohio State Medical Center where Keith was in a coma in the intensive-care unit. I spent about 15 minutes alone with him talking and crying and asking questions that I knew he could not answer. Walking out of the room, I tried to leave the contents of my brain's basement there behind me. I've realized that it doesn't happen that way, at least not for me. The misery empties, bit-by-bit, as I share my story with others. Keith died alone in a nursing home in Marion, having never fully recovered from his traumatic brain injury.

After four years at Elyria High, my body began to tell me that I needed things to change. My blood pressure was getting higher and the chronic pain that I have struggled with since high school flared up with a vengeance. I started taking medications that zoned me out, and I had to admit that I couldn't juggle this level of work any longer. One of the many horrible things about surviving a childhood like mine is the physical toll that it takes on one's body. I suffer from a few different autoimmune disorders, and they are all idiopathic, meaning no one knows what causes them.

Today I can be found supporting superintendents, principals, teachers, and parents through Ohio's statewide system of supports. Sixteen State Support Teams are scattered throughout Ohio with the role of assisting school districts and community schools in using research-based best practices to improve in the many areas schools are rated in each year. I am a member of

State Support Team, Region 2, supporting school districts in Erie, Huron, and Lorain Counties. If you have ever been to Cedar Point, the roller-coaster capital of the world, that's in my region of Ohio.

My specific role there is to support schools with parent and community engagement, and with the implementation of Positive Behavior Interventions and Supports (PBIS). Being skilled at "noticing things," I also observe teachers and teacher teams providing feedback to them in an effort to help them improve their skills in supporting the social/emotional side of educating children.

As I meet with educators across our region, I always ask them two questions: "What percentage of your daily work is devoted to the social/emotional side of education?" and "How many courses did you take in your teacher licensure work that were dedicated to training you to teach and support the social/emotional side of the children you teach?" The answers to these questions have given me some data to illuminate one of the largest issues our schools face today. Teachers report that they spend at least 50% of their days supporting the social/emotional needs of their students, with many teachers reporting 70% to 75%. The answer to the second question is usually zero. Every day we send our educators into classrooms with little or no training to perform at least half of their jobs. Should there be a question as to why educators struggle in that area?

As my career in education winds down and I look for my next calling to help others, writing this story has been the most important step I have taken toward helping myself to heal. My prayer is that through sharing my story, others will find hope and know that there is a way out of the darkness. Writing your story, actually putting it down in words takes the memories' power away. It takes courage, but it is so worth doing.

Nowadays, in my free time, I can usually be found enjoying my family. In 2009 I decided that I wanted to learn to paint landscapes. Darlene had taken a picture at a local park, and it was beautiful! I went to my art teachers and told them I wanted them to teach me to paint. Instead, they suggested a senior student who had incredible talent. During her study halls, if I had free time, I would pull out my canvas as she guided me to learn the basics of painting with acrylics. This hobby has become my therapy, and I've been successful at once again, creating things that make people, including myself, very happy!

# FROM ADVERSITY TO ART
## DARREN CONLEY

*Original work by Darren Conley*

Charlie always said, "When you write that book about your life, I want to see my name on the dedication page." Tragically, Charlie died when his bicycle was hit by a car two years ago. Charlie, my friend, I dedicate the telling of my story to you: Charlie Startup, a man who pointed out the path that would lead me on my journey to healing.

# Chapter Seven
# Out of the Darkness

*Jennifer Casa-Todd*

> *"Be kind*
> *For everyone you meet*
> *is fighting a battle you know nothing about."*
> -Unknown

*Jennifer Casa-Todd is a mom, wife, teacher-librarian, former literacy consultant, MEd student, author of Social LEADia, learner, and thinker. She has worked closely with the Bully-Free Alliance of York Region and is an Associate for the Digital Citizenship Institute. She shares her passion for student voice around technology enabled-learning. She believes we need to think critically about issues of equity, access, privacy, and safety, but that part of our role as educators is to inspire students to embrace the opportunities before them to make the online and offline world a better place.*

My childhood was fraught with adversity. I was so awfully bullied in elementary school: because I was cross-eyed, because I wore the wrong clothes, because everything about me was wrong. It led me to some very tumultuous teenage years where, because I lacked self-confidence, I made some rather poor choices.

And yet, because of those past experiences, I have often felt so blessed in my adult life. I have a wonderful husband, two beautiful teenagers and truly good and supportive friends. I look back at that time of my life, and I realize that the many blessings for which I am grateful are more evident to me because of the difficulties I have faced. I know that I am more sensitive to the students who may not necessarily fit in, and my focus on inclusivity and kindness comes to me as a direct result of those experiences. I value every connection and friendship I make because I know how awful it is to feel all alone in the world. I have worked extremely hard to become the kind of teacher and leader who inspires and supports.

When I wasn't fulfilling my mom duties or running a household, I belonged to two book clubs, curled, skied, golfed, blogged, presented at conferences, organized conferences, shared on social media; I over-volunteered and tried my best to help anyone who asked. I was taking my Masters in Curriculum and Technology and had spent the summer of 2016 writing a book! I was always DOING.

Then on October 31st, 2016 all that busy-ness came to a grinding halt.

In retrospect, I know it was because I was jet-lagged and over-tired. I had just been a part of something special: The Digital Citizenship Summit at Twitter headquarters in San Francisco. I had met awesome students and educators who I invited to contribute to the book as my deadline loomed on December 1st.

It was an innocuous door. One that I had passed through for two months in my role as a new Teacher-Librarian. But on October 31st that door would stop me in my tracks for 10 months. The impact of hitting it on the way out caused me to suffer a concussion: what I later would know is called a mild traumatic brain injury (MTBI).

At this point, you must be wondering, "Really? A concussion?" I thought that too. When I lay in bed those first few weeks unable to get up without feeling dizzy and nauseous, I felt so stupid. I had friends who had suffered from cancer with seemingly more drive than I had. The humiliation of it coupled with the inability to function fully as I had before was only part of what I was feeling. The doctor said no reading, no writing, no rigorous exercise, no screens; basically, everything that mattered to me was restricted.

While pre-MTBI Jennifer was a social butterfly, post-MTBI Jennifer avoided people. In fact, there were many occasions where I did not want to see anyone or be with anyone. At first, it was because of physical symptoms. It didn't help that I couldn't take a shower without feeling pronounced nausea and dizziness. So of course, when you avoid showering, you avoid people. I don't know how my family could stand to be in the same room as me.

The hardest part was watching life go on around me. In the first few weeks, it was a real struggle to go down the stairs.

But based on other people's stories, I guess I expected the physical and cognitive impairments that followed my injury. What I could never have imagined was the emotional impact. I felt like no one would want to talk to me because I had nothing to say. How could I? I was in bed for weeks and even missed the US presidential election. Christmas, something I always look forward to, was horrible. I was so grateful that my good friends did some Christmas shopping for me because I could not face a mall or even a drug store.

I remember when I thought I could handle a visit to a drug store for a few stocking stuffers. My good friend Pam drove me there, and when she went to look for her own items, she returned to find me seated in an aisle with my eyes shut tightly and my hands covering my ears. I had no idea how much light, noise, and movement assaults your senses in such an environment, so a mall was out of the question.

After the first month or so, the various responses to my injury ranged:

"Maybe this is God's way of telling you to slow down."

"Really, you're still not better?"

"You're not trying hard enough to get over this."

"I have a friend...have you tried??"

While I appreciated the recommendations of doctors, osteopaths, chiropractors, natural remedies, and unsolicited advice, I appreciated the silent support more. I don't mean silent, I just mean people who were patient and just listened. I have very close friends who suffer from depression, anxiety, and PTSD and have always believed myself to be quite empathetic. I try to listen non-judgmentally, and I watch the comments I make which might be inadvertently hurtful. I thought I had a pretty good handle on what and how they might be feeling. But it wasn't until this injury that I really did understand it.

My good friend, Scott kept inviting me out for lunch, and I kept saying no. When I finally agreed to go out for lunch with him, it was not the best experience for either of us. We went to a quiet place, hat and sunglasses on and I lasted about 30 minutes. I felt awful and just did not want to be with people. And I cried, no I sobbed every single day for several months. I'm fairly certain I cried when I was with him that day.

My attempt at a modified schedule at work was exasperating. Everyone was quite supportive and understanding, knowing my work ethic. I was most disappointed in myself actually; my inability to come back full-time. If I thought a drugstore was bad, a library with all the moving people and parts was like a minefield. And yet, when people saw me, makeup on and dressed in my work clothes, there was not real empathy or understanding. This is likely because I wasn't wearing a cast on my head or on my heart.

Technology was both my enemy and my savior! On the one hand, I was really limited in the amount of screen time that I could handle. On the other hand, Siri, podcasts, and Voxer helped to alleviate some of the sheer boredom of being at home with limited capabilities. Siri allowed me to "text" my family and friends as well as "read" blogs.

People always condemn social media but what they don't realize is that inasmuch as it can be a way to take away from your relationships (if you let it), it can also be a source of strong relationships that have the power to uplift as well. And although I did have to take drugs for my headaches, sleep disturbances, and sadness, I truly believe that having my friends reach out to me via social media helped me not only to stay sane but to heal emotionally as well.

My EduMatch Voxer family, in particular, lifted me out of my misery. Sarah Thomas, the founder of EduMatch, had suffered a brain injury and talking to her via Voxer helped me so much. Fellow EduMatcher Jennifer Bond suggested I watch the TED talk by Jane McGonigal (2012), aka Jane the Concussion Slayer, which basically saved my sanity. It was like I was hearing my own story being recounted for me. Her book was the first audiobook I purchased, too.

Jane's TED Talk recounted her experience with mild traumatic brain injury and her subsequent depression. Jane, a game developer, created a game called *Superbetter*, designed to gamify your recovery. I immediately downloaded *SuperBetter,* and though I don't know that it helped immensely, it at least gave me goals. Take a shower. Get dressed. Walk down the stairs. Make myself a meal.

I vividly remember my first real attempt to be myself again: Canada's Connect Conference. I had canceled three previous conference presentations and felt like if I did what I loved doing, it would help my recovery. It was in April and was a first for me on lots of levels. It was my first time as a Spotlight speaker. It was the first time my husband and I attended a conference together - though he had no choice but to come with me because I would not have been able to drive myself there and back in addition to presenting a one-hour talk. It was also the first time I spoke publicly about my MTBI by doing an Ignite.

If you saw my talk at the Connect conference in April, you would never have never known that I was in any way not my normal self. Because my presentation comes from my heart, I was able to do it some justice. You likely would not have guessed or noticed that in order to be able to present for an hour, I had to spend time before and after in my room resting because I did not have the physical or cognitive strength to do anything else. Though I was more myself a few months later at the International Society of Technology in Education conference (ISTE), being "normal" and sociable meant escaping quietly to my room to sleep for a few hours or skipping a dinner with everyone because I did not have the cognitive or physical stamina to make it through.

I also happened to have a book deadline to meet. As I lay in darkness day after day wondering how I would be able to edit my book, I was a twist of emotions: anger, disappointment, and frustration. I felt like if people in my own family doubted the extent of my symptoms, what would a publisher who really did not know my work ethic think? Thankfully I had written 95% of it the summer before but finishing the book would be my savior: my goal. With limited capacity for screen time, I enlisted the help of friends to critique it, and I remember lying in bed day while my daughters went through the edits.

They were my editors and scribes. I remember my friend, Stefanie, also coming over to work on the edits, bringing tea and treats while I lay on the couch and tried to concentrate on the words she was speaking. It was both a demoralizing time and a time of renewal because it meant so much to me that they were doing this. I finally acknowledged that I could not possibly sit at a computer with my entire manuscript and that my December 1st deadline would not be met.

I reached out to Shelly Burgess who was entirely empathetic and assured me that Erin Collins and her team would be able to do the "developmental editing" for *Social LEADia*. Hearing those words brought a tsunami of tears and relief. Because not working affected my sense of self: I did not feel useful, I poured whatever energy I had in the day to my book project, and it really helped my recovery. When it was published, albeit later than scheduled, it was a physical testament that reaching out to others for help can make all the difference.

Unfortunately, when it comes to a brain injury, sheer will can only take you so far. I know that the concussion protocol emails sat unread in my inbox, and yet the more I speak to students and teachers, the more I know that many people are affected by MTBI. It seems that at least once a week I overhear a student who is suffering the ill-effects of a concussion. I can't even imagine being a student sitting in class for six hours straight, listening to instruction upon instruction or sitting in a noisy, busy classroom and then having to go home to work on homework. Everything about a school is an assault on the senses: the fluorescent lights, the hordes of people in crowded hallways, the slamming of lockers.

Similarly, I can't imagine having so much of your social life happening online when you are supposed to limit your time on a screen. Most of all I worry about the lack of empathy of others. One young woman shared with me how hard it is because her teachers don't believe her, and, in some cases, her friends don't either because she goes on social media to stay connected. It's a double-edged sword--the longing to feel normal vs. the limitations on normalcy.

Education about what MTBI is and isn't is essential for offering support to students and colleagues. I was given the following Guideline for Concussion/Mild Traumatic Brain Injury & Persistent Symptoms by the Ontario Neurotrauma Foundation (2013):

| Sleep/ Energy | Thinking/ Memory | Physical | Emotional/ Mood |
|---|---|---|---|
| Sleeping more than usual | Difficulty thinking clearly | Headache | Irritability |
| Sleeping less than usual | Feeling slowed down | Balance | Nervousness |
| Trouble falling asleep | Trouble concentrating | Blurred vision | Sadness |
| More tired than usual | Difficulty remembering new information | Dizziness | More emotional |
| | | Nausea or vomiting | |
| | | Lack of energy | |
| | | Sensitivity to noise or light | |

It was amazing to me when I saw this chart as it made me feel like I hadn't gone crazy; that other people were experiencing the same things I was. Not everyone feels all of these symptoms and not to the same extent, which is why someone offered, "Well So & So had a concussion and was fine in a week." I think that's the greatest difficulty for MTBI victims.

I share this information far and wide because people with MTBI need support and understanding. This is why I created a quiet space in my library with natural lighting. When I was recovering, I offered a meditation session during lunch, a ritual that continues with a co-teacher today. I also have a space to color; a simple yet powerful thing that allowed my brain to relax and so many students come to use that space to de-stress. I am connecting with our guidance department to offer my support as I want to use my experience to share with both students and teachers whenever I can.

I spent years at the district level showing teachers how to use assistive technology with all students; especially students with specialized learning needs. "Good for all and necessary for some," has a whole new meaning for me now. Google Read and Write, Siri, even the voice feature on a phone can provide so much reprieve for students and help them to participate in some activities. These are accommodations that can be made very simply but can make all the difference.

Today, I still feel the occasional brain fog when I am pushing myself. It serves as a reminder that I can't do it all. When I do overextend myself, I can recognize the trigger (a squeezing of the brain feeling) to go and rest and try not to feel guilty or self-deprecating when I do: feeling well means listening to my body. I know that my perspective on life has shifted, knowing that in a blink of an eye your life can dramatically change. When I walk into a room that has too much going on like bright lights or lots of peripheral movement and noise, I do my best to reduce it. I think this is helpful to all learners not just people suffering from MTBI. I definitely tread more cautiously and move more slowly. My greatest takeaway is to remind myself that among us are teachers, students--people--who are experiencing stress or trauma or tragedy or mental illness which we know nothing about because they look perfectly normal.

# Chapter Eight

# Career Atrophy and Healing Process Driven by Two Index Fingers

*Rick Jetter, Ph.D.*

> "Nearly all men can stand adversity,
> but if you want to test a man's character, give him power."
> -Abraham Lincoln

*Rick Jetter, Ph.D. is the co-founder and partner of Pushing Boundaries and can be found by visiting him at www.pushboundconsulting.com and www.rickjetter.com. Follow him on LinkedIn, Facebook, and Twitter at @RickJetter. You may call him at 716.860.0380 or e-mail him at drjetter1@gmail.com. He will get back to you right away and will be honored to meet you and know you.*

## The Mythical Ladder of Success

I didn't realize my own warped interpretation of career success until my career crumbled to the ground. I loved teaching my seventh and eighth-grade students when I first began a career in education. I worked hard to get there. Straight A's in college, loads of references from people who observed me teaching ELA, colleagues, and supervisors pulling for me to get a teaching job within a saturated market consisting of thousands of certified teachers with only a handful of jobs available each year. The colleges and universities in Western New York were pumping out so many talented educator-phenoms. I believed in myself. Many told me that I had a unique and special talent. A great presenter. A great speaker. Sharp dresser. Cool guy. Smart and confident.

After year number five of teaching, I started to crave something different. I was getting a little bored with my classroom even though I enjoyed my students. I just thought that there was more out there for me and I naturally thought that I should be looking for more. Being tapped on the shoulder by my principal for considering positions of leadership, I just thought that preparing for administrative positions was my next step within the hierarchy of what I thought it meant to be a successful educator. More money. More power. More glory. More respect. More opportunities I would have to motivate and lead others. At least, that is what I thought. I saw others around me doing it, so why couldn't I move towards higher ranking positions?

## CAREER ATROPHY AND HEALING PROCESS
### RICK JETTER, PH.D.

So, I went back to college after my first Master's Degree in English Education and quickly secured my administrative certification and CAS degree in Educational Leadership and Facilitation. These degrees were framed in my house and admired by all, especially me. My wife, Jennifer, sacrificed time, money, and support for me to continue my schooling in so many ways: this was not the first time in our journey where she gave up so much for me to pursue my own dreams of what I thought I needed to do to make it in the field of education.

I became an Assistant Principal of a middle school in the same prestigious school district near my house a few months after finishing my administrative degree and passing all of my state exams with flying colors. The story of this position is about the same as when I was a teacher. After year four of becoming an assistant principal, I started to crave something different. I was getting a little bored with the position and knew that I could run my own building, especially after getting a small gig within the district as an interim principal of one of our elementary schools while I was still an assistant principal.

It was a three-month gig while the principal was out on maternity leave, but I just thought that there was more out there for me and I naturally thought that I should be looking for more. Everyone told me how talented I was. Teachers. Parents. Supervisors. Bigger dreams. Bigger goals. Climb the ladder some more.

I became a principal of a K-6 school in a neighboring district, four miles from my house, a few months after realizing my desire to, again, move up the ladder. I had so many new on-the-job learnings. I experienced some adversity with my PTA and a few teachers at that school over issues that I thought I was right about and that they were wrong about. I had a vision to spill in all sorts of technology to support instruction, and this was where I wanted to see all fundraiser monies go. The PTA wanted to throw parties, celebrations, field days, and buy students prizes, and other stuff. We disagreed about our philosophies regarding what was best for the children. Since I wasn't successful at trying to work things through, after many failed attempts to bury the hatchet with the PTA leadership team and get back on track, I decided to look for a new experience even after receiving tenure because I naturally thought that continuing to move up the ladder (to a central office position) was what I needed to do, anyway.

It was what I thought was next. Don't get me wrong, I had it pretty good as a principal, but I was still never satisfied with where I was because there was more, hierarchically in my head. I finished my doctorate while being a principal. This was yet another sacrifice that my family made as Jennifer continued to be my number one supporter. Now having three children, I wanted to give my family more, and I believed that my talent would get us more.

I became the Assistant Superintendent of Technology and Human Resources in a new, neighboring school district months after my decision to start looking for a new job that I thought would bring my family and me more and more good fortune. However, this position was a landmine in disguise the moment I was approved by the school board.

With litigation taking place due to a tape recording of a particular executive session regarding discussions about terminating an employee, my superintendent faced extreme adversity each day. He was battling the terminated employee's family members and friends who finally acquired seats on the school board. As a result of the chaos, a special meeting was called on July 1, 2013, and my superintendent was placed on administrative leave for the remaining days of his contract even though he announced his retirement before the election. They asked him to turn in his keys, laptop, and other district property immediately and leave the district.

So, everyone looked to me for riding out this treacherous storm and fighting a battle which many believed needed to be fought. I was supposed to save the district from a string of ongoing litigation related to a new decision that I had to make: placing a tenured teacher on administrative leave who was close to the very same board members who defended the termination of the previous employee. The war now became "nuclear," and there suddenly were no rules being followed for common civility among opposing forces.

I was appointed as the Interim Superintendent of Schools and shortly after, without my wife's knowledge or blessing, I applied to become the Superintendent of Schools even when the battles were increasing in severity on both sides. I was going to fix that place I thought, when in fact all that I did was crash and burn. The community looked to me to fix everything. The staff trusted that I would bring peace to the tumult.

I will never forget the day that I was appointed as the superintendent of that school district. I received a standing ovation from the audience and while I shook hands with community members and parents, staff members and students, I thought to myself, "Oh my God...what did I just accept?" I was already dying inside with fake smiles pasted to my face on the outside. My Superman syndrome took over, but I wasn't going to catch Lois Lane with a happy ending. I ended up dropping her.

When I look back on my brief superintendency, I didn't have the wisdom, emotional intelligence, or health to prevail as the superintendent of schools in that particular school district at that particular time under those particular circumstances. I felt like there was a beehive over my desk each day. My health was declining, my marriage was an afterthought to my work, and I forgot what my children looked like.

The process of removing a school board member by attending nightly legal hearings was suffocating me. I worked 15-18-hour days just so I could beat them and win the litigious war on behalf of the school district. I was depressed, pumped up on all sorts of prescription medication for high blood pressure and anxiety, and I burned through vodka bottles like they were bottles of water. Nothing could stop the pain. I wanted out and even wanted out of more than just my job. *I wanted out of life.*

I remember sobbing at my desk filled with legal papers and looking up at the sky outside of my office window begging God to "get me out of there." Overwhelmed with my own stubbornness of wanting to save that school district, my own mistakes, and the revenge and shrapnel that I battled each day from various school board members and community members who were part of their army, I checked into a hospital in order to heal and recover on so many different levels, both mentally and physically. I later resigned as the superintendent of schools only after one year and three months.

The top hierarchical position of being a superintendent of schools isn't always a nightmare. I know that. There are many great school districts governed by many great school board members and amazing superintendents. But in my own unique experiences that I'm not sure you would even believe if I told you, it was a living hell. My professors never taught me about that in school after four degrees with over fifteen years of undergraduate and graduate work. This was the school of hard knocks. Casualties existed, people were villainized on both sides, and war felt like it was the only option especially when litigious swords were drawn on the battlefield. Lawyer up or die. With personal interests driving my adversaries' attacks on me, children were forgotten - and I'm disgusted and embarrassed to say so.

## The Healing Process and My Index Fingers

> *"Mindfulness is about love and loving life. When you cultivate this love, it gives you clarity and compassion for life, and your actions happen in accordance with that."*
> -Jon Kabat-Zinn

After my release from the hospital in August 2014, my wife and I became reacquainted. We played tennis while the Jetter kids were at school. We worked out together at a local gym. We ate lunch together, laughed, and cried together. I learned about how I would never make decisions in a vacuum ever again. I learned more about my love for Jennifer even though the journey of healing had more ups and downs after I left public education. Experiencing PTSD and healing is still an ongoing process for me, but my healing all began when I started using my two index fingers to write my first book, The Isolate /n./, which is a novel about an autistic 6th grader who gets bullied by his classmates.

See, Jennifer gave me space to write. She knew that I had these ideas in my head and my writing was a form of mindfulness and healing for me. It kept my mind off of the bad stuff. The haunted memories. The stress that I felt. I had lots of nightmares. Writing would make me happy again. Jennifer was so caring and still is. She fought for our family, and I owe her my life. She let me do what I think I now do best: write.

## CAREER ATROPHY AND HEALING PROCESS
### RICK JETTER, PH.D.

I can't even begin to describe to you how I feel when I write. Words talk to me through my fingertips. I feel energized. I feel alive. I feel like I still contribute to the field of education in new and amazing ways that I would have never pursued in my previous position. Writing feels like a drug. It is a high for sure. I can actually feel my juices flowing. I can feel the creativity pouring from my fingertips. Those two index fingers of mine. I never mastered keyboarding.

So, after I wrote the *Isolate /n./*, I wrote another book entitled *Sutures of the Mind*. Then, I started opening up on social media. I started using Twitter, LinkedIn, and Facebook at first to market my books, but then to really learn from educators all over the globe. I never knew what Twitter chats were. I never studied the art of connecting with others on LinkedIn until my world opened up wider for me. This is how I met Rebecca Coda. She saw the cover of Sutures of the Mind on LinkedIn, bought it, read it, and sent me a message thanking me for my work--that it was helping her to get through a tough time in her career, as well. We started talking, then became co-authors, and then became friends and business partners ever since.

I loved writing so much that I wrote another book entitled *Hiring the Best Staff for Your School*. Next, Rebecca and I hit the scene with a book about adversity in leadership entitled *Escaping the School Leader's Dunk Tank*. Then, I wrote another book about student narratives entitled *Igniting Wonder, Reflection, and Change in Our Schools*. Then, another book flowed through my index fingers with Rebecca Coda entitled *Just*

119

*Ask Them!* which is about student voice. Then, Jennifer Fraser looked me up on Twitter, and we wrote a book about bullying and neuroscience entitled *Brain Scars*. Then, another one ... and another one ... and another one ... they are all in my head waiting to come out. There are more books to come. So many more. This is just the beginning. Writing is my new antidepressant medication. I'm addicted.

Feeling Arizona

> *"Feelings are at the basis of all ideas. First, you have feelings, and then, through those sensations, it develops into ideas."*
> -Jeff Koons

Speaking engagements for some of my work started to trickle in. Then, a few engagements started to pour in. To date, it has been a wonderful ride that I have been on. I didn't realize that people wanted me and Rebecca or me and Jennifer, or just me, to speak about my work and train educators on what I have researched and what I know about best practices in education or forward thinking with students at the center.

It only recently hit me in October 2017 when Rebecca and I presented at the 2017 BET-C Conference in Phoenix, Arizona. I decided to go swimming in the hotel pool upon my arrival in Arizona the day before we were going to present our work on *Escaping the School*

*Leader's Dunk Tank* and *Just Ask Them!* I love the sunlight. I can't get enough vitamin D. I remember looking up to the sky while enjoying an amazing sunny day and thinking to myself, "If adversity in my career did not happen, I would not be here now. Thank you, Lord."

I felt the hot sun of Arizona and my faith flow through my veins. I was alive again, and no one was going to bury me. Not yet, at least.

## 10 Lessons that Adversity Taught Me

> *"The growth and development of people is the highest calling of leadership."*
> -Harvey Firestone

As I train school leaders and educators about so many exciting topics in education, especially about adversity in education, I am fortunate and honored to take the talents that God gave me to follow through with doing good work in schools across the nation to help both children and adult learners. From "living hell" to "living well," I always share some of the things that I have learned about myself when I tell my story.

The following 10 lessons are universal. They apply to both traditional and modern schools. They stand the test of time. They have been written about by others, I'm sure, but they have a special place in my heart as I cling to a hopeful future that is filled with new opportunities to help others. In no particular order, my notion of battles, wars, and adversity within my career have taught me to:

1. Be humble and grateful for everything that I do have.
2. Realize that being right is not important.
3. Forgive others even if it takes time-- sometimes, even a *long* time.
4. Understand that a job is just a job. A career is just a job. There are more important things in life.
5. Reflect on how wanting attention isn't about others. It is about you and needs to be reflected on and channeled back to being humble.
6. Be content and honor contentment because it doesn't mean that you are static, not learning something, or not growing.
7. Know that you can't control that which isn't in your control.
8. Leave any job that doesn't bring you some sort of happiness.
9. Know the difference between money and power versus good fortune and service.
10. Stop. Pause. Breathe. Reflect. Readjust. Rejuvenate. Rekindle. Refire. Stay hopeful.

I needed to learn each one of these tenets of prevailing, both for my own personal life and professional contributions to the field of education since 2014 when my career crumbled, and I started writing and publishing to help others navigate the landscape of politics in education.

We *can* explicitly teach students about adversity and prepare them for maybe not *all* but some of the experiences that they will face (because we will all have so many different, varied experiences). But, what we *can* teach our students and staff is how to better work together with one another, how to cope with difficult situations, how to analyze where we are and how we are changing (sometimes for the worse), or just simply how to get out of situations that are unrepairable. Quitting doesn't mean failing and experiencing adversity doesn't mean defeat, either. I'm honored to be called upon by schools and organizations all over the nation. I am grateful for these experiences.

## Gaining (Some) Strength Again

> *"They tried to bury us; they didn't know we were seeds."*
> -Mexican Proverb

I am not any kind of a best-selling author. I am not a NY Times best-selling author. I am not financially wealthy because of my writing. I am not famous for my writing. I am not a highly acclaimed, high priced keynote speaker. I am not known in most places, but I am fortunate to be invited to some places. And you know what? I'm doing OK. I'm an underdog, and that's OK with me too. I'm writing for pleasure and for service to others.

That's my *greater* accomplishment. I can still put cereal on the breakfast table for my kids. But now I get to watch them eat it before I head into the office. That's a remarkable victory for me in itself.

The subtitle of this section includes the word "some." I won't lie to you and tell you that I've left my past behind me, that I'm fine with what I'm doing and where I'm at in my life right now, professionally. I've had to repair my digital footprint every single day due to nasty hate blogs and inaccurate media stories that reported my downfall. I'm sure potential employers locate me on Google and become disgusted. Little do they know that the media slant that was taken against me is missing about 45% more details that wouldn't vilify me any longer. I've had offers to tell my story, but I declined them all. It is what is best for my family and me.

I still have bigger dreams and dreams about making a comeback in my field. Yet, that swinging door back into the school system may very well just stay closed for me for a reason. Either way, I won't fight what I am meant to do. I'm putting my faith in God to let him drive my course. See, he listened to my plea for help when I was a lost superintendent asking him "to get me out of there." I may not have enjoyed how he got me out of there, but he lived up to his word.

Don't get me wrong though, the whole thing still hurts. I blame myself for so much each day--mistakes that I wish I didn't make, energies that I wish I saved for other more important work that would help children. Sometimes the memories of my experiences creep up on me without warning. I think back to all that I invested in myself, all that my wife and family sacrificed for me, all of the preparation that it took to work with children and educators within public school districts, and I sometimes get really down when thinking about how I'm not there (in schools) any longer.

I'm either *told* that I am over-qualified when searching for new opportunities or I'm *not told* that I come with too much baggage. The invisible, faceless, judgmental personnel decisions that others make saddens me the most. If only they would invite me in to let me tell my story. Then they could decide if I am a terrible person or a stronger, smarter, and healthier leader - now more than ever before. The educational community can be very unforgiving, and many school districts across the nation do not embrace adversity, making mistakes, or experiencing defeat. They want to appoint those with squeaky-clean records of flawless service. I get it. I really do. But, maybe those who have gone through adverse situations can offer more than those who don't experience adverse situations or make mistakes.

I don't know. I'll never truly know the answer to that. *What I do know is that I'm a better person now than I was then.* I'm a better judge of character. I'm healthier. I'm more reflective. I'm more balanced. I'm a better husband. I'm a better father. I'm still giving back to students and educators in lots of places in ways that I never imagined. I am proud of how far I've come. I do believe that what I'm doing and where I'm at is just another pit-stop in my life journey. But, you know what .

. . I'm content and OK with that too. I don't have a mythical career ladder in my mind any longer.

I'm also pretty sure that this chapter has helped me in my own healing process even if my career atrophy took place over three years ago. If you look back at Table 1 again, my immature outlook on success seems so crooked. Boy, did I have a lot to learn. Maybe extreme adversity and career atrophy were meant to make me come alive and help others all at the same time? I'm certain that this book will assist others to reflect on their personal and professional lives and equip others to be the very best educators for our students--educators who talk about adversity and strip down the myths that distract us about learning what life is really all about.

Identity is always in the making, but I predict I will only get better, both personally and professionally, as a result of the adversity I faced in my career. We are seeds. We are all seeds when adversity creates havoc in our own world.

# Chapter Nine

# Dueling the Parent and Educator Role as an EDvocate

*Rebecca Coda*

> *"Holding on to anger is like grasping a hot coal with the intent of throwing it at someone else; You are the one who gets burned."*
> -Buddha

*Rebecca Coda, M.Ed., NBCT K-6 Director of Curriculum & Instruction. Author of Escaping the School Leader's Dunk Tank & Let Them Speak, she serves as a social justice warrior, ambassador of hope, futurist, national speaker, founder of Digital Native Network, and co-founder of Pushing Boundaries Consulting LLC. Rebecca dreams the impossible and believes anything can be achieved through focus, collaboration, and a growth mindset. She can be reached via her website at www.rebeccacoda.com or follow her on Twitter: @rebeccacoda.*

## Being a Parent and an Educational Leader

As I sat in the meeting clicking my pen at the rate of an automated factory machine, my heart began pulsing faster and faster. My anxiety was increasing, and I knew I was nearing a panic attack. As Penelope from Saturday Night Live would say, "It was a panic 'anic' attack" (because that is even bigger). Thank goodness my husband was in the IEP meeting with me because I was so angered that I stormed out of my own son's IEP meeting. After I had already responded, I knew this was a knee-jerk reaction to my past experiences. You see, I've always had to advocate and fight for my kids when the educational system had failed them. It even reached a point that I had to hire an advocate on my child's behalf because the system was failing him. Needless to say, my own fight or flight kicked in, and I chose to flee without looking back. [Mistake #1]

When my emotions took over, I made a direct exit to the door as fast as I possibly could. In the hallway, I bent over and took a deep breath, so I didn't pass out. Tears welled up. I felt that the situation was hopeless. And then fear set in. My own child who was adopted from the foster system, who has reactive attachment disorder, dyslexia, dysgraphia - wasn't going to be helped by the public school system, again. I feared this lack of attention to his needs was going to be another factor that would stack the odds against him, again.

He was expected to sit up quietly in rows and complete boring worksheets without accommodation (other than being told to "get to work"). His IEP was gloriously written and had accommodations like fidget tools, sensory breaks, a cool-down room, manipulatives for conceptual understanding, an emotions communication sheet, and the strategy of chunking the work into smaller parts. But it wasn't happening. The story gets even messier if I go back to the beginning of the situation.

## The Beginning

As the newly hired district technology integration specialist, I had the luxury of observing teachers through the lens of school improvement and effective instructional implementation, which most parents don't. During the first weeks of school, I had a routine walkthrough scheduled at my son's school. I had already walked several of the elementary schools and found it such a joy to see kids having fun at learning stations, and engaged using laptops, interactive student notebooks, flexible seating, anchor charts, vocabulary supports; I saw Pinterest-perfect rooms, routines, a culture of mutual respect, and sensory accommodations for all kids. They were happy learning environments that evoked a true love of learning, giggles, and high fives. This idyllic scene of positive intent was swirling around in my thoughts as I entered my son's school. Boy, was I blindsided.

That day, we were participating in school-wide walkthroughs for inter-rater reliability, and I was joining our curriculum director and the other content specialists from the district. On that day, in the very first classroom we entered, we saw blank walls and students in traditional rows sitting straight up perfectly poised to avoid getting called out. With the exception of the teacher lecturing, you could hear a pin drop in nearly every classroom. Students were compliantly taking notes. It was sterile. Nobody dared to flex a muscle, or they would have to face the consequences that were hanging on the wall on the "red" chart. The demerits were very clear, and nobody dared to get singled out. Room after room, kids were sitting silent, doing silent work, and being actively shushed by any adult in the room demanding compliance.

As a leader of student engagement and innovation, this made my heart ache for kids, and I was devastated that this was their learning environment. We went in several more rooms.

*Then we entered my son's classroom.*

Instantly, his eyes locked onto mine and they were pleading helplessly. He looked guilty and desperate all at the same time because he knew he was caught disengaged and not doing his work. He was emotionally shut down. I stood in the back of the room waiting to see how the content and inclusion teacher would respond.

The teacher announced that they were to solve the math problem on the Google Doc electronically. At first, this piqued my interest because the teacher appeared innovative in integrating technology and allowing students an alternative to worksheets. He even walked the room with a strut, seemingly proud that he was caught using technology. At first glance, I was thrilled that students had this relevant opportunity. But at a closer look at the actual activity proved different.

Students were allowed no paper, no manipulatives, not supports, just solve the problem, 10 ½ - 4 2/3=, and type in the answer. This was the expectation for all general education students, as well as the eight special education inclusion students in that classroom.

The eyes of desperation, frustration, and failure gazed back and forth among students too fearful to ask for help and only allowed to silently type a response. It was now obvious that this attempt at integrating technology (which is to be commended) failed epically because it was just an electronic version of packets that were happening school-wide. During this paralyzing event, the inclusion teacher leaned over and whispered to my son, pointed to his computer and walked to the next student and did the same thing.

I watched this hovering and pointing inclusion strategy take place with each and every inclusion student. There were no strategy reference tools, no manipulatives, no scratch paper, and definitely no reteaching in small group at the back table to support conceptual understanding. I was so devastated that I, too, was paralyzed. One of the other content specialists even leaned over to me and asked if it was the gifted and talented class because the work was so inappropriately high, and no supports were evident.

Needless to say, the drive back to the district office was somber. We met back in the curriculum conference room to debrief. My director first asked us what we thought. The others began with a few small compliments like, "The kids were well-behaved. They had good note-taking skills."

131

Then I shared just how devastated I was as a parent and as a kid advocate. The other content specialists said in unison, "We feel so bad for the kids."

The next part of conversation moved to, "What are we going to do about it?" My director shared that it was an isolated walkthrough and that we would need to go back and visit again to see if it was an anomaly or if this is what school looks like for these kids every day. We scheduled another date to go visit again.

Week after week, our site visit kept getting bumped due to other scheduling conflicts. My director had encouraged us to drop in when we had time, since it was going to be too hard to schedule a time we could all visit again. One afternoon, I had a cancellation and had some free time, so I checked with the others to see if they could go. They were booked for the afternoon, so I decided to just go on my own before any more time got away from us. [Mistake #2]

I popped in and out of classrooms, and to my surprise, several classrooms had hands-on activities going, and some classes had students engaged in talking. This was a delightful improvement from the last site visit. Not perfect by far, but a big difference from the last visit. Then I entered my son's classroom. When I entered, the lights were dimmed, the teacher was at his desk, and students were silently working on worksheets. The teacher came over to me, asked if I was looking for my son, and I said, "yes." He shared that he was pulled out and across the hall with the inclusion teacher. I had completed my observation and went into the hallway to see the inclusion teacher returning with my son. He beamed and was excited because he had completed his timed multiplication worksheet. The teacher was proud of him.

The inclusion teacher explained how well things were going and how responsive he was to his positivity. While we were talking, the general education teacher walked over to get the worksheet for my son. He held it on the edge of the table, ripped it in half, and put it down on my son's desk. You see, one of his accommodations in his IEP is to have his worked chunked into smaller parts and only receive one problem at a time, or he would have an emotional response.

My blood began to boil as I watched this scenario taking place out of the corner of my eye. Not only did he not plan for an accommodation, but he was also merely complying with the IEP because an adult of accountability was in the room. This situation oozed of either incompetence or disrespect. My heart wanted to cry for my son who was set up to fail, and I couldn't save him, I had to walk out the door and leave him in the situation. I was fixated on leaving the room as quickly as possible because my mom-meter was blaring warning sirens loud enough to reach another dimension.

As I headed for the door, I lowered my tone in almost slow motion and told the inclusion teacher, "I am so angry right now I am going to have to leave." [Mistake #3] I left without another word.

Although all my emotional responses were justified, and it was okay for me to feel the way I felt in the heat of the moment(s), the choice(s) I made in response to those emotions lacked wisdom and left me grasping the hot coals. I created a lose-lose situation not only for my son, but also for all the other students I was advocating for. In retrospect, I could have made this personally heated situation a win-win situation for all kids if only I had set boundaries in place.

I did my best to repair the situation by visiting with the principal, first apologizing for my behavior and second, sharing why I acted the way that I did. I was able to switch from wearing the parent hat to wearing the hat of a content specialist. I didn't sugar-coat anything and stuck to the facts I had written down: students were not engaged, there wasn't a positive learning culture, and students with IEPs were not receiving the level of support they deserved. I offered my full support through walkthroughs, coaching teams of teachers up, and even writing improvement plans for teachers if necessary. The students deserved more. They deserved an advocate and a newly drawn expectation of excellence.

---

*Lesson #1:
Always have an exit plan.*

---

As humans, we are biologically emotion-driven creatures. This is both a blessing and a curse. Even though my intent to advocate for special education students (especially as my son) was on the forefront of my mind, my responses were fueled by resentment, anger and disappointment of the present and the past. These were my feelings, and there was nothing wrong with these feelings, but I entered my son's IEP meeting described at the beginning of the chapter already amped up and emotionally charged. I should have been prepared for what I would encounter at the meeting. But I wasn't.

By walking out without addressing the situation or my reason why, I was left looking ignorant and incompetent. If I would have had an exit plan that communicated my "why," I would have exited the room with credibility. Instead, I left my husband sitting there high and dry. My emotions were valid, my thinking was valid, but my response to adversity was not appropriate, especially as a leader within the district. I should have been prepared with an exit strategy that sounded like this: "I am not going to be able to continue this meeting right now because I am so emotionally charged by the tone of this meeting and my prior observations. I need to step away from this situation so that I can collect my thoughts. I apologize, but I must excuse myself, and we will need to meet another time."

*Lesson #2:*
*Always observe with another person.*

Any time you know you need to observe any classroom for any reason where there is any possibility for adversity to arise, always bring someone with you. Whether you are observing a classroom with your own child, a teacher that can be confrontational, or a classroom that may require a courageous conversation, always bring somebody with you. If I had my content specialists with me the day that I observed my son's classroom alone, I don't think I would have told the inclusion teacher that I was angry and stormed out. I would have had another adult to see what I saw, validate behaviors, and document.

---

*Lesson #3:
Never walk out communicating
disapproval. Make a graceful exit.
Always.*

---

Similar to Lesson #1, simply walking out is a cop out, but walking out with disdain and disapproval was even worse. I never should have put myself in the position of going in alone, unprotected. And although in the moment I believed I was communicating the reason for walking out, it made things even worse. Both teachers were oblivious that they had even done anything wrong; this form of teaching had been acceptable and was part of their culture. Because the math teacher and inclusion teacher were simply doing their job and carrying out what was expected, they were blindsided that I would be so angry at anything they had done. They didn't know what they did wrong, while at the same time I felt paralyzed and trapped in the moment.

Regardless of my feelings, I should never have put myself in this position in the first place of going in alone, I shouldn't have walked out, and most importantly, I should not have communicated my disapproval. This only potentially hurt my son even more.

As an instructional leader, this closed every possible door for coaching these teachers in the future or igniting any kind of passion for learning and growing. It turned into a battle. In that final heated moment, my simple reply should have been, "Thanks for your time, but I am going to have to run for now. I hate to cut you off, but I'm going to step out, and I'll have to follow-up with you later." That would have conveyed neither approval nor disapproval, and would have provided me time to step away and deconstruct the situation to come up with an objective game plan before re-engaging in a conversation.

*Lesson #4:*
*Even if you mess up, good things can still happen.*

Even though I failed epically as a parent and district specialist in my "Edvocate" role (which is harder than being an advocate), there was still good that came out of this situation. By sharing "why" I stormed out of that classroom with the principal, it painted a clear picture of who I am as an educator. When the principal understood that I acted the way I did because of my prior experience with a failing system, that I was a passionate and dedicated educator of high-quality instruction to all, somehow this painted a noble picture for him. These were good reasons, and he understood.

The principal took copious notes as I shared the areas of improvement that were needed school-wide. He even asked me for the names of those teachers that needed most improvement so that he could pay closer attention to those classrooms first.

He seemed to take this as a challenge to improve rather than defending their ineffective practices. I was grateful for the conversation and for clearing the air. I steered clear of this campus for weeks just to let things settle down. One day, I finally sent a calendar invite to visit the classrooms again as a follow-up with two of the other content specialists. I was prepared to experience the same dissatisfaction as before, but this time I was prepared for adversity. I was braced for it, I had my peers alongside me, and also had an exit plan in place in case classroom instruction was just as sterile. I took a deep breath as I entered my son's classroom guarded by my troupe.

To my surprise, I experienced something like I've never experienced in all my years of education. It wasn't even the same recognizable school. Students were actively playing fluency games; there was student-to-student interaction. They were high-fiving, smiling, and thriving through learning. The morphing that took place on that campus was night and day.

That day, I felt guilt: guilt that I had been so hard on the principal, but then I also felt reflective gratefulness that he had taken the high road and rose to the expectation because of it. The principal shared with me that there was initial resistance from some teachers, but once he finally broke through, they were willing to try new practices. And they did! It made all the difference.

## DUELING THE PARENT AND EDUCATOR ROLE AS AN EDVOCATE
### REBECCA CODA

Whether you are a teacher, principal, district leader, or parent leader, the bottom line is that we all have the power to influence. As a teacher, you may deal with emotionally-charged parents on a routine basis, many times unjustified. Being able to have an exit plan, knowing when to bring another adult to a meeting, and never communicating disapproval will always leave you with grace and the power to influence. Parents know their child best, and any teacher-parent conflict requires acknowledging and understanding their point-of-view.

As a principal, there are times when teachers may leave you drained. Your feelings are valid, but you must take action as their leader. Holding an ineffective or toxic teacher accountable can be the breeding ground for adversity. Any time a teacher is unaware of their ineffectiveness and is held accountable to a new and higher standard it can create an environment of dissonance.

Always having an exit plan, knowing when to bring a colleague for observations to cover yourself, and never leaving an observation with a comment of disapproval are essential. Anytime you face a difficult meeting, your exit plan could include an unbiased script of evidence that can help focus the conversation on the evidence rather than on feelings toward each other. Difficult post-conferences should always be well-planned and never communicated in the heat of the moment.

As a district leader, I will ALWAYS have an exit plan, observe every classroom with another colleague, and exit with grace - no matter what my emotions are telling me. Everybody deserves their dignity. Everyone deserves to be understood. No matter who is right or wrong, or if adversity is a product of unfortunate events; no resolution will ever evolve without objectivity and understanding.

That day in the IEP meeting I felt like a failure as a parent and doomed as an employee. I didn't even have the skill set to say why I was walking out; I just walked out and didn't return. At that point in time, my actions exhibited both disrespect and disapproval with no possible hope of reconciliation. The arrows all pointed to me because I didn't have an exit strategy to leave that classroom with a positive tone and grace. In retrospect, if I had known then what I know now, I could have prevented adding fuel to the fire of adversity. Adversity is inevitable in every facet of life. Don't get caught grasping the hot coals like I did. Choose to have an exit plan, have someone alongside you, and always exit with grace - especially when you are an *Edvocate*.

# Chapter Ten
# Overcomer Teacher

*Melody McAllister*

> *"Hardships often prepare ordinary people for an extraordinary destiny."*
> -CS Lewis

*Melody McAllister is the Garland NAACP Teacher of the Year 2017. She is a proud parent of five beautiful children and the wife of an incredibly dedicated man. Teaching for more than a decade, she believes there is always something more to learn, and her faith helps her in all these aspects of life. She loves building her Professional Learning Community, so follow her on Twitter @mjmcalli and on LinkedIn.*

Mid-July 2015, I was in a lawn chair outside with my four children watching them play, contemplating how our lives were in their present state. A week earlier, my husband, Mac, had pawned my wedding band, and we had taken out a title loan to cover groceries and our mortgage payment. In previous years, we had cashed in my teacher retirement and sold a rental home two separate times to bail us out of debt. Had we not learned anything? The dream of homeschooling my children and being a stay-at-home mom vanished into the air, and I knew what I needed to do.

Resigning my teaching position not quite four years prior, my former boss assured me she'd welcome me with open arms if I ever wanted to return and teach at her school. I took a chance, as my teaching certification hadn't expired, and asked her if she had any positions open for me? Two weeks later, I had a fifth-grade teaching position at my former place of employment. Adding insult to injury (or confirmation that we badly needed another paycheck), one of our vehicles died a tragic death the day before I went back to work.

Thankfully, I had a faithful friend and colleague who was more than happy to pick me up every day for those first two months until I received my first paycheck to get work done on our car. Those talks with Patti on the way to school bolstered me back into my former profession, and the humility forming my life was taking root. My oldest child and I started school in the fall of the 2015-16 year at Carver Elementary, she in the first grade and her momma in the fifth. I had no idea how much I'd be schooled that year!

Getting back into the classroom came with some perks, too. When my first paycheck finally came in, we used it on the down payment of a 2008 Sonata. My daughter really enjoyed school, and I looked forward to a decent Christmas after years of not being able to afford much. Two incomes instead of one was a luxury we hadn't had in years. However, on Christmas Eve my husband received notice of an impending layoff, and this blow totally did me in. I questioned the faith I had in myself, God, and my marriage, and I started to wonder if I was doing anything worthwhile? But that was just the beginning of my unraveling. Doubts assailed me on all sides. Should I have even gone back to work? Was God punishing me for taking matters into my own hands?

The last two months of my husband's job as a radio frequency engineer in a telecom business took him traveling in other cities and states. The fear of being by ourselves without him gave way too many sleepless nights. That's truly when survival mode kicked in. I lived on a 24/7 supply of coffee and sugar to get me through each day. When his job was finally over, we tried to make it on my income and his new job as an Uber driver (thankfully the Sonata was new enough to allow him to do this). He received six months of unemployment, but we never had enough for our family of six. Our health insurance was so expensive we felt we had no choice but to let it go.

Until then, it seemed we could always bail ourselves out of any financial troubles before it became a crisis. Until then, even in the worst of our conditions, we still lived a pretty blessed life, but we were starting to see life through a different set of lenses.

By that spring we found out I was pregnant again. It may seem ridiculous, but this increased my anger towards God--how dare He allow this to happen when we were so broke?! As desperate as I was, you'd think the next thing that happened would please me. During the first day of state testing (we had just officially confirmed our pregnancy that morning) I had unbearable cramps and all the signs of a miscarriage by lunchtime. I missed the next two days of school and testing. I was barely able to confess to my team what happened because I believed I was to blame for this baby's death through my poor diet, my anger, and stress. My students were confused about why their teacher would just leave them on such important days.

Though I tried to keep my cool for my family and students' sakes, depression settled in. When I wasn't busy trying to be everything I was supposed to be for others, I was crying uncontrollably, cutting people out of my life, and falling into a dark hole. No surprise that my students' science scores were lower than the previous year with the former science teacher. I felt like a failure in every aspect of my life. I just knew my principal regretted hiring me back; how could she feel any other way? I had let everyone down. These thought patterns were on repeat in my mind.

It's funny how certain memories get stuck in your brain. You can remember everything clearly; I'll never forget those moments of doubt and questioning every decision we had made. In the beginning, I really did think it was an answer to prayer to go back to work. I thought it could even be temporary if we climbed out of the money pit [again]? But "this answer to prayer" was nothing like I expected.

We had no idea that just around the corner, my husband would be laid off from his job and that eventually, the stress would lead to a miscarriage and depression. If we had known the future, I never would have considered going back to work. But upon much reflection, the most challenging days became the catalyst that would begin to shape me into a better person, wife, mother, and teacher! The power of connection became my way out of the dark hole. I used that superpower the next school year to connect with my students and help them focus on their growth, which is the most important piece of the puzzle in the learning process. So maybe it was nothing like I expected, but it was everything I needed, and my faith began to grow as I learned how to forgive myself and let go of the anger.

Life really is a series of ups and downs, don't you think? There are definitely events we can control, but many we cannot. *Embracing* the toughest of times is what helps us grow through our experiences. On the flipside, *avoiding* those times makes life even more difficult, and the challenges may build up into something we feel might break us if we don't get help! It can be quite humbling to realize that our students face these same kinds of setbacks. For instance, they don't always come into my fifth-grade classroom on a fifth-grade reading level. Many of them are being traded between their parents' houses or apartments any given day or week. They suffer from anxiety, even at the ages of ten and eleven. They struggle with abuse, being bullied, ADHD, or other illnesses...sometimes from all of the above. Life isn't easy for any of us when we start thinking about these details.

What pulled me out of my depression was finding how to reconnect with people who understood what I felt and giving a voice to my pain. I didn't know how to do that at first, but with each conversation I had with an empathetic friend, I realized that everything I felt and struggled with mattered. Helping my students put a voice to their obstacles and showing them how much I cared was how I was able to connect with them in their own struggles. This was a very important part of the growing process for all of us.

It can be exhausting to be a teacher on a good day, but what do you do when your life is a mess, and not all of your students have what they need when they enter your classroom? Here are some things I learned....

You meet each child exactly where he is at that moment. You don't sugar coat her problems. You teach them how to meet new challenges by leaning in and working harder than ever for the sweet reward we call growth. You cannot help them achieve this without a powerful bond or connection. As an educator, rushing on to cover the next unit when your students aren't alongside you is too costly if your goal is to see growth. Because I had grown stronger through my personal challenges, I was able to see and connect with their fears that threatened to keep them stagnant.

The superpower of connecting through struggles is very real. The year following my financial problems and miscarriage, that's the mentality I had as their teacher. Connection strengthens the influence a teacher can have on her students. Can't read well? We're going to work on it. Feel out of control without your meds? We're going to work on it. Don't know how to multiply? We're going to work on it. Give up when one doubt assails you? We're going to work on it. Most importantly, feel left behind, and everyone else is moving forward too quickly? We're here for you, SO DON'T QUIT!

This superpower of connection and bonding shaped my classroom culture strongly and positively. We were super quirky, but by the end of that year, we were truly exhausted and proud of the progress we made-- even when we felt the challenges were too tough at times!

The year following my miscarriage gave me a grit I didn't know I possessed. Perhaps holding on for dear life showed me that many of my students were doing the same. The difference is that I had more coping skills in my arsenal. Wasn't it my duty to help them increase theirs? And that's exactly what we did.

We talked through ugly battles and fights. Three girls who were accustomed to nasty drama and friendless lunches and recesses told me that never could they remember a teacher sitting and talking with them about their issues. The conversations we had were real, brought tears, and forged deeper relationships. These girls had to be vulnerable to move on, and boy did I know how that felt! It only cost me one lunch break, roughly 25 minutes. But those 25 minutes increased learning time throughout the year, and invisible walls were torn down.

We set goals to help keep us accountable for not giving up when it was much easier to avoid the work or go back to old behavior patterns. I made sure to connect and work with parents even more than I had in previous years because as a parent myself, I knew my kids needed me more than anyone else. My students needed their parents and teacher to be on the same team. It was going to take a family, so that's what we became.

The year following my miscarriage showed me how to celebrate life. Celebrate every wonderful moment: every goal achieved, every win, every time we worked tirelessly and saw growth. This is a part of connecting and growing together, too. My students' parents helped me in this process, and it became an extremely memorable year for all of us. We were a community.

We were even featured in a *CBS This Morning* news story about a program we used called Flocabulary. Flocabulary chose our class because of the supportive classroom culture we possessed. The culture that we grew into and celebrated came through all of us pushing and reaching for something more - that is, pushing and reaching for something more *together*.

The year of healing illustrated how the connectedness with my students allowed me as their teacher to know when to move forward, stand still, or go back according to what each child in each struggle required. We don't all go at the same pace. From the year of hurdles, hurting to healing, I developed an ability to reach my students and help them where they were struggling the most. Whether their obstacles were based on academics or were social-emotional, we worked through them together as a family.

First, we addressed the issue by name. Then we talked about it plainly, made a plan, and lastly, reflected on any growth or pitfall. There are setbacks in life and in learning, but we can use this time of adversity to grow our abilities to connect instead of shrinking away from our source of help. I taught a message of hope that stuck as my fifth graders left our classroom community. They know they have a choice when it comes to leaning into those hard lessons instead of quitting and never facing them at all. I hope they are so proud of their own growth that it propels them to accept every challenge with grit. I know this is exactly the spirit that helped me reach them in their weakest moments.

On the day of our fifth-grade commencement celebration, a father and mother with tears in their eyes came and thanked me for all their son had achieved. See, their son was a class clown and was used to just getting by, but he certainly had many gaps in his learning that scared them for his future. By the end of the year, this father was amazed at his son who sang a solo in front of everyone, who passed his state tests on the first try, and who had grown so much he barely recognized his namesake. He asked me, "What did you do that helped him so much?"

I was moved by his emotional display and had nothing but honesty to answer, "I am so proud of Julian. He worked so hard this year, and I was hard on him every single day. I would not let him give up, and I would not let him give me anything less than his best." And that's the truth. I adopted this attitude for each of my students and watched them rise to the challenge.

The year after the biggest financial setback we had ever experienced, I saw what it was like to be in the sweet spot of life. I learned to appreciate the road to success as much or more than the actual success...to appreciate the pain that leads to unexplainable joy. I experienced it, and so did my students.

If not for the experience of grief and setbacks that life doles out, I would never have known this joy. I know connecting with family, friends, and my faith in God are what pulled me out of my darkness, and that is what helped me reach out to my students. I hope they continue to build on what I taught them throughout every aspect of their lives. I hope they never settle or become comfortable as victims of circumstance. As a teacher, I will never let any future students settle for what is merely comfortable or mediocre. My students taught me that high expectations through powerful, connected relationships can defy limits!

The year anniversary of my miscarriage is when I found out we were expecting again. Joy! Joy is what my heart felt and still clings to when I don't have all the answers. When I feel afraid for the future, joy is what brings me back to the present. A year after my miscarriage I was nominated and unanimously voted as our local NAACP Educator of the Year 2017. Never expecting any recognition more than what was already clearly seen in my students' faces, that kind of recognition brought so much more joy because it came through the hardest year of my life. It was the year when

I chose to connect and see it through - even when it was a daily, hourly, minute by minute decision to keep moving forward.

Adversity can teach us more about life than the sweetest of victories because the mountain tops only have room for a few people at a time, but the slopes and valleys can hold us all. Imagine every individual holding the hand of the next person pulling them up as they go. This is what connects us and makes us real to one another. This is the reason I am able to build strong relationships with my students and their parents. This superpower is the very foundation upon which everything else I do rests. Firmly, I stand in the belief that nothing in this life is wasted, not even the ugliest parts - especially not the ugliest parts! When we connect with them, our faith, and the people around us, it gives us a supernatural ability to stand and grow when at first, we want to give up.

So where are we today? Mac and I celebrated the birth of a baby boy, our little, rainbow baby, in December 2017. Mac was finally able to hang up the Uber keys for a different career path, along with leadership roles. A new set of dreams for us both has helped me realize that whatever happens in life, personally and professionally, I make a difference.

Real life can't be escaped, and I refuse to live in fear of the future or its challenges. Our students and their families have the same roller coaster lives, but that doesn't mean we can't all make it out or use it to propel us into a dimension of greatness we've never experienced. We always have a choice to give up or stand up. We are better for each challenge we face if we choose to grow through it and take as many people up with us as possible. In my darkest moments, I never thought there would come a day when I would appreciate these challenges and the person I've grown to be through them. But, I am more than grateful.

**The Storm**
*By Maxim Grubenko (age 14)*

*A storm had come*
*for which its goal was to destroy*
*All the threads that we hold dear*
*It takes away all our hopes*
*And leaves, only dark, empty holes*

*It comes without notice*
*It leaves just as fast*
*Almost as if a second passed*
*It leaves us worried, it leaves us torn*
*Without a clue as to where we wronged*

*It leaves us with just one shred of fabric*
*which tells us*
*That we must learn.*
*to change*
*to accept*
*And that we must learn that not all is lost*

*You can gain what you lost*
*And if you can't then don't forget*
*That if you come down this path again*
*you won't make the same mistake.*

# Chapter Eleven
# Educator of Steel

*Jarod Bormann*

> "The greatest compliment that you can give anyone is to let them know that you listened."
> -Unknown

*Jarod Bormann is an Instructional Technology Consultant at the Keystone Area Education Agency in Iowa. He is also an adjunct professor for the Instructional Technology Master's program at the University of Northern Iowa. Prior to his current role, he was a middle school/high school English teacher and was recognized as Iowa Safe Schools Educator of the Year in 2014. He has been named one of the Top 40 Flipped Learning Administrators and Tech Coaches Worldwide by Flipped Learning Global Initiative, and he's the author of Professionally Driven: Empower Every Educator to Redefine PD.*

A three-year-old boy with a tuft of brown hair runs across the living room at the speed of light with a red towel tied around his neck. It wildly bounces off his heels as he runs and jumps from one piece of furniture to the next. "It's a bwird...it's a pwane...it's Supaman!" he shouts proudly. After testing out his new "cape" and super speed, the boy feels compelled to now go save someone. "I heaw something." He stops in the middle of the living room for his super hearing to adjust. "It sounds like someone is in twouble!" He quickly grabs his cape and throws it behind him as he dashes toward the couch. He leaps with two feet and lands. Before making his next move, he says, "Don't worry, I'll save you!" Then he tears off towards one end of the sofa and leaps once again with both feet off the arm of the couch. Like Superman when he flies, the boy puts out both arms and the rest of his body parallel to the floor. Superman flies...three-year-old boys do not. Realizing gravity is taking over, the boy attempts to brace his fall with his hands but instead ends up in the ER with a sprained arm.

***

My arm healed just fine, but as far back as I can remember, I've always been drawn to Superman - his story, what he stands for, how he works to bring out the best in people. This ideal was instilled early, and it would carry through to my years in education - *the idea of possessing a superpower that could bring good to others and maybe even save some.*

Some might say educators have superpowers. Maybe it's unbelievable bladder control due to restricted bathroom breaks or a heightened sense of patience when a full moon is present. Are educators born with these superpowers like Superman or do we obtain them through some freak accident like Spiderman? Every great superhero has a backstory...and this is mine.

***

Some months after my first and only attempt at solo flight and ensuing ER visit, my parents divorced. I do not remember the day or the moment my mom, three-month-old brother, and I left Florida and came to Iowa. My mom remarried the man I call my dad when I was five. I always called him Dad. I even consider my two sisters that came after the new marriage my genuine sisters. We grew up on a farm in small-town Iowa, raised sheep, did what normal families do. I wrestled, played baseball, football, 4-H, choir, showed sheep, school plays (at least for one year), and made National Honor Society. If you did not know me before the age of five, you would swear my family was a normal nuclear family from the Midwest.

While going through school, my biological father and his parents still had visitation rights once a month and on certain holidays. I don't need to draw out the details of these visitation years spanning from my lower elementary days to eighth grade, but there was animosity on both sides, to say the least, and my brother and I were caught in the middle. This eventually led to a court battle over visitation rights. While the case was in court, my brother and I were court-ordered to see a therapist during these months, and this is where I was diagnosed with clinical depression as a 7th grader. "Also, your biological father is gay. Do you know what that means?" the therapist asked me in one session. I nodded my head yes even though I barely got over what he just said. "Now, we don't know if homosexuality is hereditary or..."

He went on to explain further in medical terms what being gay means, but I stopped listening after he nonchalantly alluded to the uncertainty of gay genes being passed onto offspring. As a seventh grader, I was already in the midst of my most awkward phase of life both physically and socially. Trying to find the daily balance between being a model student with just enough smart aleck comebacks to keep me in the top half of the popularity ladder was daunting enough. Now, I had to question my DNA makeup. My friends said I have nice handwriting. Did that mean I was gay? My two best friends since kindergarten were girls. Did that mean I was gay? At the last middle school dance, a few people said I was a good dancer. Did that mean I was gay?

Before my therapy session was done, I had mentally run through every gay stereotype that I knew of and compared that to my own daily habits to see if there was some sort of scientific correlation. *My biological father is gay, and I think girls are cute.* That's the only real seventh-grade conclusion I could come to.

When the diagnosis of depression was revealed, the court battling stopped as well as the visitations. I would later find out that it was my biological father's decision to do so because he was fearful of how emotionally damaging it was on my brother and me. I went about my high school years seemingly normal to the public eye - Clark Kent amongst the citizens of Metropolis. However, like Clark, I would be carrying around with me a secret about my past. No one back at my school or even my town knew of my biological father, or the fact that he was gay, or that I was diagnosed with clinical depression. And there was no way I was willingly going to tell someone either, out of fear of being socially ostracized.

\*\*\*

"Are you ok?" was all the email said. It was from my biological father. I had not talked to him since 7th grade. He wrote to me after some riots took place on my college campus. Seeing his name in my inbox after six years startled me, and I froze for a good few minutes when I read his three-word email.

"I'm fine," was my only reply. Emotions began to swirl as soon as I hit the send button. I stood up from my chair in my tiny dorm room, put my coat on and said to my roommate, "I'm going for a walk."

He looked up from his homework puzzled. "Now? Why?"

"I got an email."

"From who?" Like all the guys on my floor, he was an engineering major. I was the only English major. I proofread a lot of his papers for him, but I didn't have time to correct his grammar in the moment.

"My biological father," and then I shut the door behind me.

\*\*\*

It was some time past 10:00 PM and the Iowa temps were near single digits, but I needed to make sense of what I was feeling. Mainly confusion...some frustration. Why is he contacting me after six years? I thought he didn't want to see us anymore? Can't he just leave me alone and let me live a normal life? I didn't ask him to come back in my life. The emotions and questions turbulently swirled within me.

As I continued to walk away from my dorm and into a suburban area, I tried to logically sort what I was feeling. I took each abstract emotion one at a time and tried to sort them into compartments, but it wasn't that easy. And the more difficult it got, the more upset I was becoming with myself. Why can't I control what is being felt? The lack of control within me was building my frustration intensely. I came across a small park and sat in one of the empty plastic swings. Maybe being still would help. As I sat, something began to change.

At first, I thought I was becoming calmer and emotions were settling. But then it went beyond that. It went further south to the point where I became void of the previous emotions. I wanted to make sense of them, feel at peace about them, but now I felt like they were completely drained from me. I sat on the frigid swing in a suburban area late on an idle weeknight feeling like Dante's lowest depths of hell - trapped, cold, still, and void of feeling anything, like I didn't care about anything. My anger at myself left no energy to feel anything or even care.

A car slowly approached, and I recognized it right away. My high school sweetheart, Jackie, who lived across campus pulled up in her Alero and didn't bother to roll down her window. Instead, she parked it, turned it off, and came out to sit on the empty swing next to me. I could see her warm breath in my peripheral as she broke the silence. "I called your dorm, but your roommate said you went for a walk. He said it has something to do with your biological father." Even though I went to high school with my roommate, he didn't really know about my biological father. "I've been driving around trying to find you." She didn't speak with an angry or dismissive tone; she spoke with empathy.

"I got an email from Mark." She knew who Mark was. She's actually one of the few who did.

"Saying what?"

"Asking if I was ok."

I was on the other side of campus at Jackie's when the riots took place. It was a campus-wide celebration that got out of hand and police force was used to break up the large-scale drunkenness. It made Good Morning America, which is how Mark found out. I didn't even know the riots occurred until I saw them on the news the next morning.

"Are you...ok?" I could tell she wasn't asking about the riots.

"I don't know what I am. At first, I was confused, then frustrated with him, then I was frustrated at myself for not being able to make sense of all this, and then I was getting upset at myself, and now I just don't care." I continued to stare at the ground as my breath pushed up on the light from the streetlamp above.

"What do you mean?"

"I don't know what to feel. I don't want to start up a relationship with him because it seems like it would just be easier without him in my life, like before. I mean...when we get married someday, do we tell our kids that I have a biological father when I already have a dad?"

She sat for a few seconds. "Well, I think it's our job as parents to surround our kids with people who love them. If he treats our kids with love, then what's the harm in that?" Jackie knew all about my past, she knew about Mark, but she'd never met him. "Has he ever hurt you?"

"No."

"Has he always been respectful?"

"To me and my brother, yes."

"I know divorce can sometimes be ugly, and I'm not trying to pretend like I know what you went through, but it sounds to me like you were caught in the middle of something bad. But now that you are on your own, you have the choice: accept those that love you and reject those that don't." That's why she is my Lois Lane. When emotions feel too abstract and unsortable, she simplifies them. Superman deals with turmoil around him, but Jackie helps with the turmoil inside of me.

"It's freezing. Can we go now?" she said with a smile. I didn't quite smile back, but we did get in her car, and she dropped me off back at my dorm.

\*\*\*

Three months later I proposed to Jackie. Over the course of the last three years of college, I would start a dialogue with my biological father, marry Jackie, visit Mark in Florida, meet his partner of 20 years, and realize their relationship is no different than mine and Jackie's. Seeing them happy made me happy.

However, there was still something intangible that seemed to block consistent happiness for me. Every few months since seventh grade, I was hit with these lulls similar to what I felt sitting on that swing back in the park my freshman year of college. They were these moments where staying sheltered and alone felt normal simply because it was easier than trying to explain to someone why I didn't feel like talking, smiling, or even feeling anything at all. I would come to call these moments *bouts*. These weren't moments when I felt depressed; they were moments when my depression would take over, and it really felt like I was battling against myself to stop it.

When I'm experiencing a bout, I use writing to help make sense of it. I don't pretend that I'm writing for the Daily Planet, but writing does help that sorting process of emotions, especially writing poetry. Poetry lends itself well to battling bouts because I can put concrete images to abstract emotions. The pencil is my heat vision, carving into the paper. But most importantly, I hone my superhuman hearing skills as I listen not just for alliteration and other poetic sound devices, but as I listen for connections. Am I attaching the right concrete image to the right abstract thought and emotion in order to make the right metaphor loud and clear? Metaphors help make sense of my emotions which helps win the battle against the bout.

\*\*\*

# THE FIRE WITHIN

In my second year of teaching in a rural part of Iowa, I had the opportunity to teach a Creative Writing class. Since it was an elective, there were about 15 students, and the class was a mix of freshmen through seniors. I was more than excited to start the poetry unit. There was one student, a senior named Dylan, who seemed to be quieter than the rest. He had more introverted tendencies which I recognized because I also tend to be more introverted. As they were working on some writing one day, I walked past this student's desk and noticed that he had a notebook full of poetry. "Do you write poetry in your spare time?" I asked.

"Yeah," he said quietly.

"I love reading poetry. Anytime you got a poem you want some feedback on, I'll be more than happy to read it."

He nodded his head slightly. "Ok."

\*\*\*

The next day, Dylan handed off a poem at the end of class. "Awesome! I'll give a read and leave some feedback. Am I allowed to write in the margins on this one?" I asked.

"Sure," he replied.

I had prep next period and decided to give Dylan's poem a read. The overall tone was darker. Not in a sinister way, but in an isolated way. Images portraying being blocked off from others as a sense of protection. I read the poem as a whole and left feedback about possible line breaks for emphasis, more concrete word choices, and other poetic devices. I also left a few comments about how I interpreted some of the images such as, *your main character seems very isolated. Is this by choice or is this the doing of the rest of society?* I was careful not to imply that the main character could be, in fact, him. I gave it back to Dylan the next day at the beginning of class and said, "Thanks for letting me read it. Let me know if you have any questions about my feedback."

\*\*\*

Two days later, Dylan handed me another poem. "Here ya go. Thanks for your feedback." Again, I gave it a read and made similar feedback remarks regarding poetic devices, but the tone and theme weren't quite as dark in the sense of shadowy figures. There were still images of isolation such as the main character's long hair being described as a cloak from others. Dylan did have longer hair, so it was difficult for me not to make that correlation, but I still didn't want to assume.

I again left comments about my interpretation of his poem and the less dark tones. I handed it back to Dylan the next day and said, "There's some good stuff in this one. Thanks for letting me read."

Again, about two days later, Dylan hands me another. The tone in this one was much brighter than the others, and it was evident that there was a shift happening from his first poem. I was glad to see it happening. Rather than a theme of being closed off from others, it was a theme of opening up and allowing more light to shine. However, using my superhuman microscopic vision, I was noticing a consistent image showing up: the hair. In the first poem it was used as a cloak, but now the hair is pulled back signifying a pulling back of the veil so to speak. It was evident that the hair was attached to a sense of identity. I left my poetic devices feedback and even commented: *Really like how the main character is opening up more and being more positive. You can definitely tell this shift over the last few poems.* I handed it back to Dylan the next day at the beginning of class, and we proceeded as usual.

Dylan did not hand me a poem the next day, and I really thought nothing of it. However, I did discover something sitting on my desk at the end of the period. It was a folded-up piece of notebook paper with my name on the outside. I had received thank you notes from students before, but not ones anonymously left on my desk. It was my prep period, so I picked it up, unfolded, and began to read. However, this was more than just a thank you note. "Dear Mr. Bormann," it started and then went on to express a crush towards me. As I read more, I gained the sense that the writer was not sure how to express these feelings any other way, but hoped I would understand. When I got to the bottom of the note, it was signed...Dylan.

I sat back in my chair a little perplexed. At first, I asked myself, *Did I - a teacher, husband, and father - somehow give Dylan the wrong impression with my interest in his poetry? Was a comment I left on his work misinterpreted somehow?* I didn't treat Dylan any differently than the rest of the students in the classroom. If any other student in the class wrote poetry in their free time, I would have offered to read it too. I believe the difference here was I was using my superhuman listening skills to truly hear Dylan, something he may not have felt before due to his longer hair and introverted tendencies. By me reading his poetry, it's possible he felt valued and this created conflicting feelings for him. The change in his poetry made sense now, but my x-ray vision didn't see it at first.

Because I'm a teacher, that makes me a mandatory reporter. I took the note to my building principal. He read it a little wide-eyed. There was nothing explicit, just an expression of feelings. When he finished, he sat the note on his desk baffled for a moment. He looked at me hoping I might have something to say. "How do you want to handle this?" throwing the ball back in my court.

"Honestly, I'm not mad or disgusted in any way. I just think he's trying to figure out who he is and writing his feelings down was the best way he could do it. Sharing them with me, however, probably wasn't the best way of going about it, but I think it's better than keeping it all bottled up. Would you care if I just talked with him?"

The principal didn't know what other options there were. "If you feel like that's the best method here, that's fine with me, but you should have another adult at the table when you talk. For liability purposes." I nodded my head and thought the special education teacher who is in my room during that period might be my best option since she is another set of eyes and ears in the room. After explaining the situation, she agreed.

***

The next day, I asked Dylan to stick around after class and pulled up three chairs to form a small triangle, so we could all be a part of the conversation with no desk between us. Dylan was noticeably shaky as I asked him to take a seat. The special education teacher and I both sat down. "Hey, Dylan. I've asked Mrs. Thompson to join us for this conversation just as an extra listener in case she may hear something that I don't and maybe add her two thoughts if need be. Is that cool?"

"O...K.?" His voice was as uncertain as his shaky hands moved to push hair behind his ears.

"I wanted to talk to you about the letter that you left me on my desk yesterday." As soon as I said this, I could see a heavy look on his face that told me I confirmed any assumptions he had as soon as I asked him to stay after class. "First, I want to let you know that I'm not upset at you for writing the note. OK?" He nodded as tears began to form. "I'm glad you felt comfortable enough to express your feelings, as you long as you realize that you cannot act out on your feelings towards me. You understand why that would be inappropriate, right?"

Trails of tears made their way down his cheeks. "Is it because I'm gay?" he said in an assuming tone, as if I was disgusted by the way he was born.

I replied with an empathetic tone. "My biological father is gay. So, the fact that you're a guy who has expressed these feelings doesn't bother me, Dylan. I would be having this conversation with you even if you were a female student. It would be inappropriate to act out on your feelings towards me because I'm your teacher and you're my student. I need to make that clear."

Tears were falling from his chin. He was trying to keep up with them as he wiped them with his sweatshirt sleeves pulled over his hands. "I should have never written that note." Dylan's whole body was shaking, and I couldn't tell if it was out of frustration with himself or not. My body tends to do the same thing in those *bout* moments.

"Dylan, expressing your feelings is ok, and you should not feel ashamed for them. They are what you feel. But feeling them and acting out on them are two different things. Do you understand?" I asked again for confirmation. He nodded, still crying. "Is there anything you want to say?" giving him a chance to ask any questions if he wished, but his crying only intensified.

"I don't want to be here," he said as he looked down, shaking his head. I looked at Mrs. Thompson with a slightly concerned look on my face. She gestured back with a slight shoulder shrug, thinking that might be the end of the conversation. But because I have depression, I can hear things that others may not.

I look back at Dylan. "What do you mean you don't want to be here, Dylan? Like you don't want to be in this room?"

He caught just enough breath to choke out, "I don't want to be anywhere."

Now, because depression has given me superhuman hearing skills, I interpreted Dylan's last remark as *I don't want to exist.* That may not be what Dylan was saying, but that's what I heard. "Dylan, would it be ok if I talked for a moment? Are you willing to stay here and listen for a minute or two, and then I promise you can go?" He nodded as he tried to find a dry spot on his sleeve to continue wiping his tears. I paused for few seconds looking to gather my words.

Not sure how to start, I managed to say, "Look, Dylan. I truly believe that we are put on this Earth for a reason. I know I was meant to be a teacher because I absolutely love every day of it, and I get to help students discover their passions. I know in this class you have expressed an interest in being a massage therapist. That's a profession that can have a profound impact on people. People will come to you physically hurt, maybe emotionally hurt too, and you will be able to bring them comfort and assuage their pain. That's powerful stuff, Dylan."

His crying subsided, and I could tell he was listening. "Right now, you may feel emotionally uncomfortable, and it may be hurting, but I know you will use this to be a phenomenal massage therapist one day and bring others comfort when they hurt." I paused to see if Dylan would respond. He did...with a slight head nod as he continued to look down. "Dylan?" He looked up. "You were put here for a reason, ok?" He nodded again. "As far as I'm concerned, everything is fine between us, ok?"

Another head nod.

"Tomorrow's going to be another great day for class. I'll be your teacher, and you'll be my student, right?" A more reassured nod. "Ok. I know Mrs. Thompson probably has some things to do, and I need to go let the principal know that we had a good conversation, and you can take your time here to gather yourself before heading to study hall. I left a pass on my desk for you. Does that sound ok?"

This time an audible reply from Dylan, "Yeah."

"Ok. Thank you, Mrs. Thompson, for joining us," I said as I stood up.

"Not a problem." She turned to Dylan. "Thanks for letting me join the conversation, Dylan," she said with a smile. He half smiled back. Mrs. Thompson and I went down to the principal to debrief the conversation.

\*\*\*

I don't know if Dylan had thoughts of harming himself or not. I never asked him. But in dealing with my own depression, I had an ominous feeling in my gut that I needed to say something, much like how Superman springs into action when he hears calls of distress with his superhuman hearing.

Dylan and I went about the rest of the semester pretty normal. I would smile and greet him just as any other student, and he continued to ask questions for feedback. A few years after he graduated, I got a message from him through Facebook thanking me for listening and helping him get through a rough senior year. We've messaged back and forth a few times just as a way to catch up. He is a stylist at a hair salon and really enjoys it.

\*\*\*

Some superheroes are born with their superpowers. Some acquire theirs through some unforeseen circumstances. Was I born with depression?

Was it acquired through ongoing trauma due to an ugly divorce? I'm still not sure, but in my quest to understand it better, I have discovered that I am better able to empathize with those that others have labeled as, "the socially awkward ones." I feel like my depression has given me superhuman listening abilities where I can hear the quiet student, the loner, the aloof one constantly drawing or writing. Those students have a voice like any other; it's just harder for some to hear them.

    Since I was three with a red towel tied around my neck, I've always been drawn to Superman - his story, what he stands for, how he works to bring out the best in people. This ideal was instilled early, and it has carried over through to my years in education - *the idea of possessing a superpower that could bring good to others and maybe even save some.*

# Chapter Twelve
# Courage Over Fear

*Jana Scott*

> "Courage doesn't mean you don't get afraid.
> Courage means you don't let fear stop you."
> Bethany Hamilton

*Jana Scott, M. Ed., a current third-grade teacher, began her teaching career in 1993. A naturally encouraging leader, she serves as a district grade level facilitator, School Site Council team member, Facilities Master Plan Stakeholder team member, and as administrative designee at her site. Jana is a lifelong learner, passionately nurturing a growth mindset approach in her students. She can be reached via her website at www.janalynnscott.weebly.com or follow her on Twitter: @janascott43.*

It started out like any other day at our elementary school. At lunchtime my student teacher, another teacher on my team ("Lizzie"), and I decided to run out for frozen yogurt. I also needed to grab items for the root beer float party my students had earned. Lizzie drove, and we grabbed frozen yogurt, made a quick stop at the grocery store, and headed back to school.

As we were approaching our school, suddenly two police cars came flying up behind us with lights flashing and sirens blaring. Lizzie slowed, pulled over, and we all felt a little concerned. But, soon a wave of relief flooded us. We saw a man at the corner near our school flagging for the police to turn right just before our school. I remember thinking, "Whatever is happening, thank God it's not at our school!" We noticed a man down on the ground, two men holding him down, and the police who had flown past us were stopping there to assist.

As we pulled into the school parking lot, the eeriest silence had fallen over our campus. A playground that should have been alive with laughter, squeals of joy, and hundreds of children running and playing was completely empty and silent. I remember the three of us noting this on our way into the staff lounge and thinking how strange things seemed.

I remember entering the lounge, and as I headed to the fridge/freezer to put the root beer float items away for the end of the day, something was very wrong. There were teachers' lunches half eaten, a fork still in a small salad, and not a sound or person in sight. Suddenly our front office secretary darted in and said, "We are on lockdown - get to your classrooms!" We were stunned and headed out the back door -- clearly, everyone was in shock. (Looking back, we probably should have locked down in the office, but we felt very safe because we knew whatever was happening, the man was on the ground, others were holding him down, and the police were safely there.) Then we noticed the trail of blood leading from the playground, around the back of the office/lounge area, to a classroom down the hall.

There was a tiny sneaker there as if a child ran out of his or her shoe. It literally looked like a news file photograph in my mind. I could not wrap my head around what was happening. I remember saying (more to convince myself than anything), "Someone had a bad bloody nose!" Lizzie replied, "That could not be from a bloody nose."

I ran with my student teacher to my classroom, which was empty. I dropped my purse, phone, yogurt, keys, everything, and then turned to run to the back door of the classrooms closest to the playground. Of course, as I was pounding on the locked door, the teachers inside saw me and said they were all ok but could not unlock the door. I knew this - we had been trained many times in this. Looking back, I should not have been running between buildings obviously, but I believe I was somewhat in shock as well as thinking the perpetrator was in custody. So, we darted to Lizzie's classroom and locked down with her.

The office speaker continued to say, "Remain on lockdown." The three of us still had no idea what was really happening. Lizzie went on to her phone to Google the news, and we learned there had been a shooting at our school. It was beyond comprehension. I quickly called into the classrooms closest to the playground and spoke to teachers who reassured me my students were safe, and my son who was also on the playground at the time was safe.

I then called out to the fifth-grade buildings to learn my daughter was also safe. I knew that if this were on the news, my husband would be panicking. His entire world was at that elementary school that day. I quickly used Lizzie's cell phone to call my husband. I said, "Tom, there has been a shooting at Kelly. Brooklynn, Carson, and I are all ok. Please don't come down here - they are closing the roads, and the police are investigating."

He replied, "I'm already on my way." He was the first person on the road as it was closed, and he was rerouted to the nearby park.

I remember lying under the windows in my friend's classroom; we were so silent and still trying to figure things out, when BOOM!! Her classroom door flew open, and immediately there were two police officers with huge guns. I didn't realize I went from lying flat to pulling my legs up and being as small as I could make myself into a downward facing ball. One officer yelled, "Lay flat!" and that was when I realized I wasn't lying flat.

It was unbelievably surreal to answer the questions: "Identify yourselves!" "Is there anyone else in this room other than you three?" "Have you checked in all of the cabinets?" It was then I shuddered, realizing there could be someone hiding in this formerly unlocked room. From where I lay on the floor, I could see them open every cabinet.

Once the school had been swept, it was determined there were no accomplices to this crime, and the single shooter was in custody, the three of us darted to the office to see how we could help. Then I learned that two children had been injured, one of them being my student. Neither injury was life-threatening, and a helicopter landed at the park adjacent to our school to take the girls to Rady's Children's Hospital in San Diego.

As news spread, parents swarmed to the only place they were allowed, the aforementioned park. Because the three of us had not locked down with students in a room, we were near the front of what would become a long line of students walking to the park. Rooms were dismissed one by one, and the teacher or adult in the class would accompany the students off the school grounds, around the corner, to the area of the park that was taped off to keep parents and media back.

If you have ever watched the news and seen teachers walking students out of a building after a situation like this, you will know exactly what I mean when I say that it felt like a bad dream, like we were walking in slow motion. How could this be happening? I looked across the tape and hundreds of familiar, yet almost unrecognizable faces. I hope I never see a crowd of parents' faces again silhouetted in fear.

Once all the students were safely released to their parents, the teachers returned to one of the kindergarten classrooms for a debrief with the officers. It was during this debriefing that we realized how incredibly fortunate we really were. The shooter fired off six rounds, and when he went to reload his gun, the chamber jammed. As he fumbled to try to unjam and reload his gun, the only men that were on our campus, the construction workers that were remodeling our kitchen, saw their window of opportunity. They courageously rushed toward him even though he still had a gun in his hand. He noticed them rushing him, and he started to run.

The men split up, one chasing him across the field and one running to get his truck in case the chase went further. The shooter jumped over the fence, and one chasing him on foot also went over the fence and took him down. The other hero drove his truck right around that corner and helped take the perpetrator down quickly. This was actually the scene that my colleagues and I saw as we approached the school. We all shuddered to think what could have happened had that gun not jammed or had those heroic men not been so attentively watching for the perfect opportunity to intervene.

Our school was a crime scene, so we all had to leave with just what we had on us. I couldn't retrieve my phone, keys, purse, or anything. We had to leave our cars for the weekend so the police could do an incredibly thorough search of the grounds, including the parking lot.

The next few days were a blur, although I will never forget them. My student teacher and I went to San Diego to see our student in the hospital that night, only to be told we weren't allowed. They were tightly holding media away, but we did speak to her parents. At one point in the weekend, we all met at one of the teachers' houses to talk and try to process everything. This was the beginning step of a healing process that would take some longer than others, but that would forever mark our lives.

Students (with parental approval) spoke to officers that weekend. An officer came to our house to speak to our son. He was one of the eight or nine students chosen to testify at the preliminary trial. The support that the parents and subpoenaed students received was exceptional.

Before our children testified, the families went to the courthouse to go over the logistics of what to expect in a case like this. The students attended a "Kids in Court" session, where they entered an empty courtroom and sat in the jury box. Each child had a chance to go up on the stand and say their name and answer some fun, irrelevant questions to help them relax. They were told they would have access to therapy dogs on the stand and learned where the accused would be sitting, as well as where their family members would be sitting. They walked the students through what to expect and answered their questions. To see my young son (along with other second and third grade students) on the stand made this surreal experience start to feel more real.

Of course, I would be strong for my son and my students, anything less was never an option. I dug deep and put on a brave face. I found strength in the courage of the little ones.

Along with the "Kids in Court" session, parents were also given a chance to meet with the prosecuting team. We were able to ask questions and as much information as they were allowed to share with us, they did. I remember one understandably concerned mother saying she did not want her child to testify. The reassuring response was that we, as parents, know our children better than anyone, and we could make the decision to decline to have our children testify, and there would be no ramifications.

However, one prosecutor gently pointed out that unfortunately, our children have a memory of a gunman on their school campus, walking toward them, waving his gun, and shooting at them. That is their memory. We were told that the students who have the opportunity to testify get to sit up high and speak, while the perpetrator sits lower, shacked to the table, and does not get to speak. The attorneys said, in no way to pressure the parents, that this is an empowering and often healing action for the students in cases like this. That was helpful in making a decision that parents should never have to make.

The students went on to testify at the preliminary hearing and knew they would also be called the following year when the case went to trial.

The students and families were offered (and many received) counseling. Loving therapy dogs were on our campus for many months following, and the incident and the community began to heal. Our community surrounded our school, and we felt loved, protected, understood, and deeply appreciated.

The thing about Kelly School is that kind of support and regard is normal for the community, but for the rest of that school year, it was even more real and tangible than it had been. Companies we had never heard of before this sent the teachers all matching shirts. A coffee cart came to our school every Friday for weeks after this incident. Companies catered lunches and families in the community started "Parents on Campus," hosting parent-led games and activities for the students to do during lunch. It was a very special year of healing and of choosing love over fear.

Our administrator modeled this in such a special way. She truly thought of everything. It was a number of weeks after the incident when she called a staff meeting. She explained how she had been so concerned for the students, their families, and her staff, and that she overlooked a very important piece.

She then reached out to the spouses of the staff members. It was truly incredible the amount of care and love that we all received. She lined up optional counseling services for any staff member's spouse, as everyone was affected and processed this ordeal in different ways. The abundance of love and opportunities for healing were a gift. Carson and many other students received counseling through the Victim's Assistance program. We were on a good path and finished that school year as strongly as we could.

The following year started, and we were all waiting to hear when the trial would start. We walked strongly into that next school year, with fewer supports than the previous year, but fewer were needed. We were putting our beautiful school back together again.

Then, mid-February, the trial began. I took time off of work to sit with my family on the day Carson testified and then with my administrator the following days. We sat and listened to the taped interviews of what the defendant had planned to do to our school. We listened in detail and watched as our strong team of warriors fought to prosecute this monster for what he did to our students and our community. It was the most powerful, beautiful, heartbreaking, but empowering time for me.

I was so proud to be part of this process, to have my son's voice and my students' voices be heard to help put this man away. I even wrote a letter that I read to the judge on the day of the sentencing. I was sad that the defendant hadn't gotten help along the way, because clearly, he was disturbed. But that did not stop me from asking the judge to guarantee that this man never be allowed the freedom to do this to another school community or other children ever again.

Things wrapped up nicely, the defendant was found sane and was locked away with no chance of parole. A collective sigh of relief flooded our community. We could finally put this chapter behind us.

Oddly enough, it was then that I began having some very foreign and unexpected health issues. I had never experienced a panic attack before, but suddenly, I would wake in the night with what felt like an elephant on my chest. It was impossible to take a full breath and nearly impossible to breathe at all. I started being afraid going places, places that were familiar and even enjoyable to me.

I continued the counseling that I had started when Carson started his, but mine now went to a deeper level. My physical reactions had my counselor, physician, and family extremely concerned. Tests were ordered, and no matter what physical evaluation was run, I would pass. It was apparent to the team of professionals trying to help me that my body and mind needed to take a break. I learned from my counselor that in times of digging deep, we do OK, but in the exhale after surviving a crisis, it is not unusual for the gravity of the situation to take a physical toll.

I finished that school year and wrestled with what to do. In prayer and journaling, along with the advice of my medical doctor and therapist, it became clear to me. I submitted paperwork to my district office and thankfully was approved to begin a leave of absence.

While trying to come to terms with this change in our family's routine, we made another bold but necessary move. We sold the house in which we were living and moved into a smaller rental property that we had purchased some years prior. This house had been built in the 1940's and had no heat or A/C. It was in a different part of town, and it was an adjustment for our whole family.

I spent that first year off cocooning. My family was so sweet and understanding and didn't expect a lot of me as I waded through some dark days. I continued with therapy and joined a women's Bible study group. I spent a lot of time at home, and it was so good to just slow down.

When it was spring and time to think ahead for the next school year, I wasn't sure how I felt. My therapist wanted to be sure I was 100% ready before I re-entered the classroom, and he strongly urged me to take one more year away from teaching. I'm so thankful I followed his advice.

My district granted me a second-year leave of absence. During that year, I was able to care for my family in a way they needed and deserved, in the way they cared for me the previous year. Our daughter was in her last year of middle school, and our son was in fifth grade. Carson was still attending the elementary school where the incident happened; although we were in a different part of town, we wanted to keep him with his friends.

That October, he started having anxiety like we had never seen before. He had been through months of therapy, but this hit out of the blue. He returned to therapy to learn that our minds hide things and when familiar smells, sights, etc., resurface, we can experience things as if we are reliving them. Because the shooting took place in October, his counselor said seeing pumpkins, harvest and Halloween decorations were probably triggering the incident for him.

Because I was off work, I decided (with him begging me to do so) to pull him and enroll him in a home-school program. I home-schooled him that fall, and it was such a gift to both of us. I love teaching, I love spending time with my family, and I knew it was what he needed at that time.

That was such a special time. Some mornings we would ride our bikes to the little downtown part of our neighborhood called "The Village," taking his math book to the bagel shop. We really enjoyed those special months, and we both made personal progress.

## COURAGE OVER FEAR
## JANA SCOTT

By Christmas time, Carson felt like he was ready to re-enter the public school system and so after the holidays, we enrolled him in an elementary school that was on the side of town where we had moved. His therapist felt a change of scenery would be good, and he was so excited. He had a very successful finish to fifth grade there.

That summer I knew I would return to teaching. I felt physically and mentally prepared, but I also had a bit of insecurity. What if I got back into the classroom and started having panic attacks? What if I wasn't strong enough to resume such a rewarding but demanding job? What if I have no other options in the education field but can't give it my all?

I had done a lot of soul-searching and decided to start a Master's program when I returned to teaching that fall. My therapist also advised that as much as I loved and connected with my former staff, I should teach at a different site than where the incident happened. I knew returning to work after two years off would be challenging. I knew starting my Master's would be challenging. I knew getting to know a new staff and community would be challenging. I was nervous but excited and knew I needed to move forward with my plans.

I started teaching at the elementary school where Carson had finished fifth grade. He was off to middle school, and our daughter was starting high school. It was a busy and exciting time. I began a Master's program in administration, and within two months, we also began the remodel on the old house to which we had downsized. We have a granny flat on our property and all four of us, along with a yellow lab and two cats, moved into 640 square feet as we began our remodel.

I was feeling incredibly blessed; grateful that Carson was back in public school and doing well, grateful that Brooklynn was excited to play volleyball for her high school team, and grateful that I was feeling like myself again and back to doing what I love. In my two years away, I had forgotten how much I love being a teacher! Everything was back on track. My husband had been a rock through this entire ordeal for me, and he was so proud (and I'm sure relieved) to see me thriving in my classroom again.

Looking back, it is almost as if there was a calm before another set of storms. I will spare the details, but our remodel took much longer than expected and during that time I also learned I had cancer. Thankfully, it was caught at an early stage and two surgeries later, I was back on my feet and able to return to finish up the last two weeks of that school year.

My students were overjoyed, and it was a very special time. I finished the school year strong and proud, and then I learned I would be changing grade levels and moving classrooms. I believe we are given what we can handle, or at least what we will be able to handle through faith and grace, so I boldly began packing up my classroom as summer began.

The following year, I taught a new grade level with a new team, felt strong, and was grateful for yet another teaching experience. I finished my Master's that spring (2016) and completed and defended my thesis.

My study, appropriately titled, *An Investigation into the Strength Sources of Resilient Teachers*, was both cathartic and empowering for me.

After the shooting at our school and during my two years away from the classroom, I did not know if I would be able to return to teaching. I was so concerned with questioning my ability to return to the classroom that I gave no thought to how that situation would actually make me grow in ways that would benefit certain students.

I now understand first-hand how past traumas can revisit in the most unexpected times and places. I have always listened to students and tried to understand them, but now I have an understanding that can't be taught. I have a connection to students who have been through trauma. I can see and appreciate their resilience, which often puts adults' resilience to shame. I am a voice for students who are afraid, even if they can't put their finger on it. I know it is real, deserves to be acknowledged, and can be overcome when addressed.

My research study on resilience, coupled with current research I read on growth mindset helps me empower my students. Not only am I more suited to acknowledge their past pain, but in some ways, I can help them move forward and overcome the past failures or hurts to some extent. I had no idea that the sound of a fire drill/lockdown drill could give a grown woman chills. It has been just over seven years, and I don't think I will ever be in a lockdown drill where I don't picture those policemen kicking down the door and searching the cabinets. This helps me understand that although we

# THE FIRE WITHIN

move forward, there are memories that are strong and can keep students captive if they aren't acknowledged and heard.

Every time I hear of a shooting, my heart and mind race back to that day. Anyone who has been through that type of situation is forever bonded with those who have experienced trauma in this way. My heart goes out to the Sandy Hook families, Columbine, Orlando, and all the others whenever another story like this makes the news because I know for a split-second, they relive their trauma when they hear the news, too. When I feel my adrenaline starting, I calmly start telling myself this is just a drill, this is not "that day," I am safe, and this was planned. This helps bring me back to the present and keeps me from getting stuck in the past.

In the years following the "incident" as we call it, when we would have a drill at school, our strong warrior principal, Tressie Armstrong, would come on the speaker and gently tell the students that in five minutes, the alarms would sound for a lockdown or fire drill. She would again say it gently at the two-minute countdown and then again right before it started. She would gently say, "This is just a practice. You don't need to worry. Calmly look to your teacher."

Tressie also notified the parents of the dates of the drills in case the students who were still struggling preferred to stay home that morning. It's been seven years, and I was off campus when that alarm rang but even today when we do drills, for a split second my mind races back to that day. I breathe, I remind myself we are safe, and I find strength in going through the scenario and coming out more aware of what students may be thinking.

I want to take everything that makes me who I am: my childhood dream of teaching, my 20+ years of teaching experience, the events at my school seven years ago, my research and studying, my faith, my belief in the purpose of my journey, raising two children (teenagers now) of my own, all of life's experiences, and give back. I'm excited to see where this takes me. My fear of returning to the classroom is just a distant memory now. I'm proud of my current work and most of all, I am an effective and grateful teacher. If this journey was all to make me a stronger teacher, better parent, more compassionate friend - it was worth it. If I am fortunate enough to move into a leadership role, I am better equipped now more than ever.

My journey has prepared me to serve in other capacities as well. I'm currently our district's grade level facilitator for third grade. I'm hoping if the time and position are right for me, to move into administrative leadership. If someone had told me during my first year's leave of absence after the shooting that it was the beginning of a life-changing experience, I would not have believed it. But I have learned beauty can come from ashes, and what doesn't kill us will make us stronger if we allow it.

I've learned resilience isn't a luxury, it is mandatory. Take time to cocoon and heal if you need to, but pushing through, counting your blessings, and reaching out to others who are going through a difficult challenge will make you stronger than you ever thought you were. It is what this life is all about.

# PART II: The Science

*Maybe life isn't about
avoiding the bruises.
Maybe it's about
collecting the scars
to prove
we showed up for it.*

-Hannah Brencher

# Chapter Thirteen
# The Deep-Reaching Effects of Trauma

## Dr. Elizabeth Rogers-Doll

*Beth Rogers-Doll was raised in Montgomery, Alabama, the oldest of 4 children. Growing up with an abusive father did not seem like a blessed upbringing, but later became the essential ingredients of empathy. Beth's mother had the courage to leave when Beth was still in elementary school. Beth attended Tulane University in New Orleans and fell in love with the music, the food, and the live oak trees on St. Charles Avenue. She took her B.A. in psychology to graduate school in Chicago, where she fell in love with the bustle and beauty of the Chicago skyline. She graduated from Illinois Institute of Technology with her PhD. in Clinical Psychology, but still knew nothing. She had an ace up her sleeve, having married another psychologist, a wise and loving man.*

*Through the years Beth specialized in trauma, especially working with individuals suffering with Dissociative Identity Disorder (DID). Becoming a Certified EMDR therapist (Eye Movement Desensitization and Reprocessing) allowed her to help people make a recovery faster. Now, she teaches other clinicians how to treat trauma and how to use EMDR to help people heal. When not doing psychotherapy and consultation, Beth is busy writing novels. Her characters have DID and are bursting with resilience. Her first novel is called Parts Unknown: A New Orleans Mystery.*

## What Keeps the Flame Alive

As you read the painful but inspirational stories of these dedicated teachers, you will recognize their enduring humanity. Each voice bravely shares a story, a story of surviving inhumanity or loss. Yet each voice shares the one rock-solid strength that topples any trauma or loss. This strength is empathy. Daily, our humanity reminds us of our limited trek and our limited role in the play of life. And yet humanity has empathy, that important quality reminding us that, though we can survive the cruelty that tries to mold us into its likeness, the loving ripples we each create have unlimited potential to warm and strengthen others. How can we be so fragile and foreshortened and yet, carry the weight of others' pain, spoken and unspoken? Those who share with others tell us that it is the giving, itself, that gives them the strength.

We marvel when we hear that someone has overcome inexplicable cruelty as a child or overcome tremendous challenges to become a kind and positive force for good in the world, don't we? Those special people do not perpetrate atrocities on others, in lockstep with what was done to them. They do not molest their own children though they, themselves, were molested. They do not mercilessly chastise their children's character, as their character was chastised. And the prisons are filled with people, some of whom are acting out the multi-generational pattern of abuse and criminality from their own families. Why do some turn to the dark side of humanity, while others hold fast with the light?

The brain is adept at compensating for damage that occurs when we are young. The brain kicks in with other options when a young child is confronted with chronic neglect and abuse. We have strategies to survive and gifts that we can bank on. A very unglamorous term called mentalization explains how we avoid becoming the boogeyman or woman we grew up with. Furthermore, mentalization is a vital tool for overcoming the big and little traumas that occur in adulthood.

## The Body Responds to Adversity

Steven Porges has a complex theory about how human beings respond to the tiniest or greatest of life events. Our brains and bodies take in information through a process he calls neuroception. It is similar to the term perception. Neuroception is how "neural circuits (within us) distinguish whether situations or people are safe, dangerous or life-threatening" (Porges, 2009). My response to a terrible event may not be the same as yours. Nevertheless, each of our responses is validly our own. There are three different responses to threats that are guided by the Vagus Nerve. The Vagus Nerve is one of 12 cranial nerves that run throughout the body. Vagus is Latin for "The Wanderer," which describes how the Vagus wanders all around the body. Think of the Vagus Nerve as a tree with three different branches of different ages.

### Social Engagement Branch of the Vagus Nerve

When we lean on others, talk with others (therapists, safe parents, teachers), we are socially engaged. This social engagement system allows us to follow minute changes in posture, body language, and tone of voice. When we feel safe with someone, we may even begin to mirror their facial expression or body stance. Don't you want to offer someone who is upset a seat near you? You are offering them an opportunity to self-regulate by sitting down. The very act of sitting down is a decision that we are not in danger. Otherwise, we stand with our body tensed.

The action of conversing with someone calmly and privately assumes a level of safety as well. That is why counselors and clergy rush into a post-disaster situation –so that they can provide that calm bulwark to individuals who have survived a harrowing event. Social engagement. It is the heart of who we are, and it protects us. If you have the tools to read people, you can determine who is safe and who is not.

It makes sense why individuals with trauma histories can sometimes be excellent at "reading the room." When we tune in to others around us, we are making sense of our environment and who can be trusted within that environment. We are also living in the moment. Whether or not I was beaten as a child, my decision to be socially tuned in to others is my tool for staying grounded in my present life, which is hopefully much more predictable than my childhood.

The social engagement branch of the Vagus Nerve is the youngest branch and reflects our development to living in groups and tribes. This branch controls our facial expression, throat and tone of voice, and our middle ear. These fine movements can be read by others.

If you are walking from a distance toward another person, your body is determining whether that person is friend or foe. If that person speaks, you are expert at reading the tone of voice to identify the person's level of threat. Depending on where you are, there may be no concern, but all of this careful assessment often occurs under our personal radar. This branch of the Vagus Nerve responds to adversity by causing us to reach out to others and ask for help. When situations are safe, this branch slows our heart rate and respiration causing us to relax and to be receptive to others. When our neuroception tells us there is danger, the second branch of the Vagus Nerve is there to help.

**Fight/Flight Branch of the Vagus Nerve: Mammalian**

If I am in danger, my adrenaline, my heart rate, muscle tension and just about everything else in my body quickly skyrockets. The purpose of this excited, action-oriented state of response is to protect ourselves. The body is on alert and lets us know.

Let's consider the situation of living in an unpredictable school environment where I am bullied almost every day. I may avoid school with whatever schemes I can identify, but once I am forced to attend school, I may be in a state of panic or close to it for much of the day. I am ready for battle, I am unable to relax, and I may not have any appetite for my lunch because my digestion is shut down when I am in fight/flight mode. As we enter fight/flight mode, blood is directed away from our digestive system, sometimes making us feel queasy. When we are engaged in fight/flight response, the comforting social engagement system is inactive. We are less aware of human voices and physical safety, and more prepared for danger.

Being in a constant state of autonomic arousal is hard on the body. People who live in violent households or who live with angry addicts can attest to that fact. It is similar to feeling like one is prey. Cortisol and epinephrine are chemicals that are useful at the time but have long-term health consequences.

According to Polyvagal Theory (Van Der Kolk, 2014), we are more vulnerable to Panic Disorder and other anxiety disorders if we have endured a chronically frightening or unstable life. It is as if we are somehow always on guard, waiting for chaos to begin. We want to believe the world is safe, but our history tells us how dangerous it can be. When the source of that danger is a caregiver or parent, our sense of betrayal creates a tremendous amount of anxiety. This is how some children go to school.

This mammalian branch of the Vagus Nerve controls digestion in all its forms and increases heart rate and muscle tension throughout the body. We are more likely to take action in the form of running or fighting. This is why people having a panic attack feel a strong urge to run away or escape.

## Collapse or Hypoarousal Branch of the Vagus Nerve: Reptilian

If we cannot act to protect ourselves and help is not coming, the dorsal vagal branch of the Vagus Nerve (DVC) kicks in. Also called the reptilian branch of the

Vagus Nerve, it is the oldest branch, tied in with the brainstem and more automatic functions such as breathing, regulating our bio-rhythms and sleeping. The DVC slows our breathing and stops our digestive function in its tracks. That is why we can't urinate or defecate when really terrified.

When fight/flight mode is switched on for way too long, we lose function. When a situation is so frightening that we cannot tolerate it emotionally and physically, we shut down. We literally are frozen with fear - our heart rate slows, and our mental processes become sluggish. This state of collapse represents under-arousal, and it is the equivalent of total submission. It is what opossums do when a predator captures them - playing opossum. It is what happens when, in a raging battle, a soldier falls to the ground and cannot function anymore but is still alive and breathing.

People in a state of hyperarousal are under-responsive, in a trance state. We call it dissociation. It is a last-ditch attempt for our mind and body to shield us from horror. It gives individuals a shaky hold on reality. They may feel as if everything around them is unreal. They usually report feeling very numb and removed emotionally. And they are not connected to others around them. They are usually trapped in a shell. This state of paralysis is literally the opposite of fight/flight anxiety. And if you have ever experienced this level of shock, you may have a very spotty memory of the events that occurred. This is your brain's way of shielding you.

Individuals who have endured extreme trauma usually have the ability to dissociate from reality. They can "space out" under duress. The problem with this is the "freeze response" prevents the dissociating person from making intentional, self-protective decisions in the face of grueling strain. Instead, they go away mentally because that is what worked when something too horrible to imagine was happening in the past. Being in a dissociative state shuts down survival strategies. In fact, people with dissociative disorders, such as Dissociative Identity Disorder, often forget to eat because they do not feel hunger normally and consistently.

**Applying Polyvagal Theory to Rising Above Adversity**

The purpose of this journey through polyvagal theory is to make a point. No matter how badly I have been treated, if I can find my way back to humanity and allow myself to connect with safe others, I can come back! And if I have endured extreme stress, I can use what I know about the Vagus Nerve to stay in a more well-regulated state in my body. Also, if I can develop a lifestyle that keeps me and my body grounded in the present, I will not be numb or disconnected from daily living or on heightened alert to danger.

If I lost my child, I might spend months or years feeling a crushing depression. But, if I decide to take a real interest in the people around me, I can come back from such a loss. Or if I never could relax with my family growing up, I can learn to relax and be myself with friends who truly accept me as I am. That's the gift of social support. It allows me to connect in the present, regardless of how difficult my life experiences have been.

Teachers who have their own trauma histories bravely go into the classroom. I say bravely, because they may be unexpectedly transported back to dark memories when they see the pain of a student in the classroom. They may feel enormous empathy for certain students. Teachers encounter badly treated students in any setting. Abuse is not limited to certain income levels.

When a teacher sees a child that is timid beyond normal or appears to be numbed out emotionally or joyless, that teacher begins to consider what horrors lie at home for that child and in doing so, might be confronting their own past at the same time. They may feel the fight/flight physical response themselves. Many teachers have reported to me that they have had a flashback (very vivid reliving experience of a bad event) while teaching. Or they may simply feel a cosmic sort of connection to a particular student. Then upon reflection, they realize that the student is very much like them regarding how they behaved in the classroom when their own childhood trauma was occurring.

But, consider the child who never stops moving and rarely seems to focus for very long. We could assume that the hyperactive child has some concentration and attentional difficulties - and we would be right. Attentional difficulties are a hallmark of trauma, not just ADHD. If I have to go to school and pretend that everything at home is ok, I may be extremely restless, running away from pain. Individuals with PTSD or dissociative disorders who have been in psychotherapy with me have told me that they underwent evaluations for ADHD when in grade school or middle school, and may have been placed on stimulants as a result of those evaluations. This is not to fault their evaluators or educators. There is often such a tremendous barrier in place for a child to tell a safe adult what is occurring that, unless and even while being questioned carefully, trauma would not be known.

What of the child that is aggressive? Or the child that always seems to be angry? Is that bully being bullied at home? We all know that the answer is not always that simple. We cannot draw a straight line between what happens at home and what happens at school. But many children externalize exactly what is happening at home, often perpetrating it on other more vulnerable children.

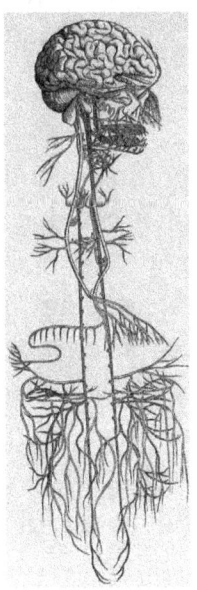

*This is an anatomical representation of the Human Vagus Nerve taken from Wellcome Library Public domain.*

## Steps to Acquiring Resilience to get through Adversity: Staying in the Light when the World can be Dark

Many good theorists and writers have written on the subject of resilience. And the research on what helps people survive difficult challenges definitely shows some trends. Below is a list of common findings and advice.

### 1. Mindful awareness of self and environment

Mindfulness is the act of consciously focusing one's awareness on what is happening in the present. It is recognizing and accepting thoughts and feelings (both emotional and physical). It is used as a therapeutic technique. It is a state of mind that many people think they can never achieve. It sounds so nice to calmly acknowledge one's feelings, thoughts and body sensations.

I prefer the definition of mindfulness put forth by Jon Kabat-Zinn, the American doctor who nurtured the mindfulness movement and the growth of holistic medicine in the U.S. According to Kabat-Zinn (2013), "Mindfulness is awareness that arises through paying attention, on purpose, in the present moment, non-judgmentally." The addition of "non-judgmentally" is what allows us to reach a state of mindful attention. Otherwise, I can sit quietly and hone my awareness of this moment, but my mind will be making judgments along the lines of how badly I sit quietly and how stupid sitting and doing nothing is. Then I think of what I should be doing instead of meditating in the moment. Before 30 seconds has passed, I will be thinking about my past or my future, but not my present.

With mindfulness, you notice judgmental thoughts and allow them to keep moving through because you are intentionally observing the moment at hand as objectively as possible. Mindfulness is the attitude that allows us to observe our responses to stress, our flaws, and limits with a beginner's mind. We accumulate so much knowledge as we grow, but we also accumulate rigid beliefs and opinions. Mindful awareness allows us to spot our dug-in ideas and allow them to dissolve.

**How We Appraise Threat and Danger**

Remember that wandering Vagus Nerve? Mindfulness meditation is making full use of the social engagement branch of the Vagus Nerve and keeping ourselves in a regulated emotional state. If we focus on now, our painful past is not a part of it. Even the difficult challenges of yesterday do not have a place in the now. Yesterday is officially over. When we feel anxious, it is usually because we fear something that lies in the future or because we are rehearsing something unnerving that happened to us. Maybe that unnerving thing happened last week. But if we embed our awareness firmly in the moment, we can more objectively respond to what is happening now. And that lovely Vagus Nerve will keep our heart rate and blood pressure even. It will also prevent the release of cortisol, a harmful hormone released under stress.

Allow me to illustrate with an example: Jack is 20 years old and is arriving at a party where he knows a few people, but not most people. Remembering painful rejections from the past, he is edgy and sweaty when he arrives at a party. His heart is clipping along when he enters the host's house. He shakes hands with the host, one of his friends, and barely looks him in the eye because he wants to hide how anxious he feels. So, he misses the warm smile from his host friend as he follows him to the kitchen where there is beer.

He passes numerous people who smile at him, but he is making a beeline for the alcohol to try to calm his nerves, so he does not stop to talk with them. After he gets a beer, he looks around and assesses the situation through the eyes of fear. He has the thought, "No one will like me." He then scopes the party for people that he knows. He stays by them most of the evening, not risking rejection by new people. He is anxious enough that he doesn't notice how empty his stomach is and doesn't eat enough food at the party, so he is drunk by the time he leaves. He made no new friends, so he did not learn new information about his capabilities socially.

\*\*\*

Let's look at Jack when he has embraced mindfulness. He is practicing what he has learned and breathing evenly. He notices that his mind keeps moving into the past, specifically to painful situations where he felt socially rejected. He notices the urge to go to the past and lets it go, pulling himself back to now. He notices his stomach growling and hopes there are some snacks to eat. He also notices a positive energy in himself at the thought of meeting someone attractive at the party.

He then walks into the house where he spots a number of smiling faces and people who begin to introduce themselves. He looks people in the eyes and asks them questions. Because he is fully in the moment, he does not misread people's faces or assign negative motives to their behavior. He doesn't perceive any psychological threat, does not think about past rejections, because he is involved with the moment as it unfolds. His heart rate stays even, so he does not experience undue anxiety. In other words, he is using his solid footing in the moment to keep painful past experiences from flooding him with anxiety.

\*\*\*

In this simple example, story #2 unfolds differently due to Jack's mindful awareness of the now. He didn't suppress old habitual thinking. He just didn't let it take top billing in his mind. He intentionally chose to notice other thoughts and feelings, like his hunger (a physical sensation that was available to him), and his positive desire to meet new people (an alternative motive and urge that was also available to him). He planned to really tune in to people to assuage those anxious feelings, and it worked.

Perhaps Jack knew that making eye contact and studying human faces would disconnect his fight/flight branch of the Vagus Nerve and prevent the autonomic nervous system from releasing adrenaline and epinephrine. Anxious, unmindful Jack was going through a tug of war between giving in to his anxiety and avoiding it by trying to repress it with beer and sticking with safe people. Avoidance is a common strategy we humans use to deal with our anxiety. The act of letting go of less desirable, judgmental thoughts takes practice, and it doesn't always work. But we are immeasurably better for having made the effort. It will pay off if we keep practicing.

**Improved Health**

There are a few other things that mindfulness is really good for. Mindful meditation lowers blood pressure, improves people's ability to fight and survive cancer, and makes chronic pain more bearable (Kabat-Zinn, 2013).

*Happier*

Mindfulness improves concentration and allows us to be more productive in order to avoid burnout. Mihaly Csikszentmihalyi (1990) researched what makes people happy and developed a theory of "peak flow" – the state in which a person is one with his/her experience. This concept applies to any activity we become one with - through career, exercise, sports or creating something. Csikszentmihalyi found that happy people spend more hours each day in peak flow than unhappy people. Here is a list of optimal conditions for achieving peak flow, from www.pursuit-of-happiness.org:

- There are clear goals every step of the way.
- There is immediate feedback to one's actions.
- There is a balance between challenges and skills.
- Action and awareness are merged.
- Distractions are excluded from consciousness.
- There is no worry of failure.
- Self-consciousness disappears.
- The sense of time becomes distorted (you lose track of time).
- The activity becomes an end in itself.

Call me crazy, but this list sounds a lot like mindfulness. Csikszentmihalyi (1990) asserted that the best memories in life were not the ones in which we are passively calm and relaxed, but the moments when we are striving to achieve something difficult, yet meaningful. When analyzing what you like about your job, try to notice what activities put you into peak flow because those activities are the ones you should do as much as possible. If you can start to observe your own moments of peak flow, they will be a source of happiness for you too. If there are too few of those moments, you may need to change how you spend your days.

**2. Empathy and Mentalization: Cultivating empathy and mentalization builds resilience in the face of unfairness.**

Teachers are often very empathetic with their students. They can visualize vividly what a student's home life is like. It turns out that empathy is a huge source of resilience. If empathy is the skill of understanding and sharing the feelings of another, mentalization is the skill of understanding the mental state of oneself and others in order to reason human behavior.

Taubner and Curth (2013) have found that people who have the gift of being able to read the thoughts and feelings of others (the ability to mentalize) are much more likely to survive and thrive after trauma. These resilient people are empathetic with strangers as well as familiar others. They fight the pull of trauma to isolate themselves and instead, stay engaged with the world. They can see the pain on another's face, read body language, and hear how tone of voice can turn complimentary words into an insult. This skill is invaluable, as it turns out.

Taubner and Curth looked at the path towards aggression in teens who were abused in childhood. Teens who could mentalize were much less likely to become violent in adolescence. The teens who showed less skill in understanding the behavior and thinking of self and others were more aggressive.

Imagine that you have no ability to reason causality in human behavior. You cannot read facial expressions or figure out why people do what they do. Wouldn't that be a difficult way to live? We would be confused and angry much of the time. Empathy is, in truth, the opposite of anger. When you turn on empathy and try to understand what makes a person tick, you are managing your own stress and strain. It becomes more difficult to judge another if we imagine that the reasons behind their negative behavior were insecurity and fear.

One of the most important gifts of mentalization is the ability to detach from another's actions and choices. When I rationalize in a neutral way why another person may have done something that injured me, I am able to distance myself from that person's choices. In other words, it is no longer about me; it is about them and what they chose to do. I can release the shame of being a victim.

This is a powerful tool for recovery from the cruelty of others. When I work with trauma survivors who hit that moment of empathy with their perpetrators, I see genuine healing. Trauma survivors who recognize the weakness and limitations of those who injured them are able to really see their own strength in surviving evil without becoming evil.

### 3. Deal with your issues.

We all avoid unpleasantness. We are pleasure-seekers, in general. But we all seek meaning as well, so even pleasure can make us feel empty when it is without meaning. If you have ghosts from your past that don't want to be buried, dealing with them is going to make you stronger and more fulfilled. That means overcoming the urge to avoid or repress pain. It could mean getting professional help from a psychotherapist or simply looking bad memories squarely in the face. No more running. No more avoidance.

Avoidance of thinking about our life's worst moments is not healthy because avoidance prevents growth. Our worst experiences teach us so much. We can learn to appreciate ourselves when we allow ourselves to think about our pain. Reivich and Shatté (2003) find that resilient people do a thorough "causal analysis" of adverse events in their life. If they find fault, they make a change. On the other hand, if the pain was caused by another person, examining that true cause will allow us to stop blaming ourselves for things beyond our control. We do have a tendency to blame ourselves when bad things happen to us, but a careful examination of difficult times will often show us how well we handled the situation at the time.

### 4. Ability to reach out for support

When we are facing adversity, it takes a village. Stress, anxiety, anger, and depression all can have the unintended effect of causing us to isolate ourselves. We feel like we need time to regroup and calm ourselves. Private time is a good thing but not in huge doses. Social support is good for regulating our point of view. Friends and family give us a reality check. If I am blaming my boss for how I function at work, a friend can point out how I can change my own behavior to be more functional.

Resilient people have a network of supportive people. We only need one person really. But if we have only one person, that individual should be the kind of person whose support is positive. When under stress, try to spend regular time with the friends who are most talented at really understanding you- not judging you or pressuring you, but empathizing with you.

## 5. Intentional Self-Care

When working with individuals who are managing high levels of stress, I always ask about self-care. It is not unexpected that I get a blank look from some clients who are strained by their circumstances. And when I say that eating and sleeping are important, I usually get a smile as if I have stated the obvious. But eating and sleeping are not natural tendencies when we are trying to stay afloat under duress. We forget to eat or our stomach rebels. We get diarrhea or constipation. We get acid reflux. And it is our body's reaction that is telling us that we are pushing ourselves to our limits.

Achieving a balance between work and play can be difficult as well. Part of taking care of yourself means knowing how you rejuvenate yourself most effectively; in other words, how do you recharge your emotional gas tank when it is on empty? Do you need time to socialize with others? Do you tend to like some alone time? Do you need to go for a run or play sports? Do you paint or create in other ways? Whatever restores your energy is important to know because it can be your lifeline when you are under high amounts of stress. Some of the educators' stories mentioned in this book have given you clues to their survival.

# Chapter Fourteen

# After the Storm: Secondary Trauma and Post-Traumatic Growth

*Mandy Froehlich*

Everyone has their own way of dealing with the fallout of a traumatic event. Some go through a grieving process, some seek counseling, some attempt to deal with it on their own with the support of others. Often traumas, such as the stories in Part I of this book, are the kind that leave lasting and far-reaching effects. Even if the trauma happened in childhood and had nothing to do with your adult profession, these effects can bleed into every part of the day including the work with children.

From an educational standpoint, two post-trauma experiences seem to be common even though they really carry very little relation: posttraumatic growth and secondary-trauma. I believe that when we are able to be self-aware and recognize certain stages we might be in, it is easier to help ourselves become better people or to deal with additional off-shooting adversities that may develop from the initial traumatic event.

Posttraumatic Growth

One of these effects is a phenomenon called posttraumatic growth (PTG). Posttraumatic growth is defined by the UNC Charlotte Psychology Department (2014) as "positive change experienced as a result of the struggle with a major life crisis or a traumatic event."

While trauma is a terrible experience and posttraumatic growth in no way excuses or eliminates the negative happening, it does explain the "superpowers" that all the contributors were able to explain in their stories. It's the part that makes us feel like our experience wasn't for nothing.

For a very specific example, in my story, I describe my ability to quickly "read a room." I needed to be hyper-aware of the climate of a room when I walked into it to determine my reactions to any mood shifts that might have been happening. I didn't even know I was doing it. When I became a teacher, I used these skills of detection with my students. I was able to quickly read their emotions as I walked in and observe where kids were and what they were doing; with a glance, I would know their moods by their body language and mannerisms. In the morning, I knew very quickly what needed to be done, so we had a great day. This skill I developed was one of my positive changes. I am fortunate to be self-aware enough to recognize it and utilize it to my advantage. This is my posttraumatic growth.

PTG is frequently used interchangeably with the term resilience, but resilience is more about the ability to recover from a negative experience than it is about the growth that results from one, although some researchers have found an inverse correlation between the two. More resilient people are less likely to experience a great posttraumatic growth due to their ability to quickly recover. Less resilient people will seek out a "new belief system" and therefore, are more likely to experience growth (Collier, 2016).

Researchers are now searching for the reason why some experience more growth than others and have found links to everything from the presence of certain chromosomes to the age at which the trauma happens. However, two traits that seem to determine a high level of PTG are the ability to be open to new experiences and the trait of extroversion, associated with the willingness to seek out support and connections when healing from trauma.

Researchers have found that PTG shows the possibility of five main areas of growth: appreciation of life, relationships with others, personal strength, new possibilities, and spiritual change (Tedeschi & Calhoun, 1996). In my example from above, I would categorize my ability to read the room as a personal strength. However, some people report seeing their lives in a new way or focusing on relationships with friends and family that they had not been before. They might find that they have a new or stronger connection with their higher power. Growth can happen in several categories and in different ways, but some people do not show growth after a traumatic event. PTG is not guaranteed, and it is not experienced by everyone who experiences trauma.

The phenomenal book *The Power of Moments* (Heath, 2017) is what originally introduced me to the concept of the posttraumatic growth, and I'm not going to lie, I was thrilled. Not because the growth makes the trauma less awful, but because I finally had a term for what I was trying to explain to people. I learned from my experiences, as did every other contributor in this book. We chose to take those experiences and use them to shape ourselves into better teachers for our students and better people all-around. As I have said, however, it doesn't make the experiences we had acceptable or welcomed. In *The Power of Moments*, the authors quote Rabbi Harold Kushner as saying:

> *"I am a more sensitive person, a more effective pastor, a more sympathetic counselor because of Aaron's life and death than I would ever have been without it. And I would give up all of those gains in a second if I could have my son back. If I could choose, I would forego all of the spiritual growth and depth which has come my way because of our experiences.... But I cannot choose" (p. 267).*

This quote encapsulates what I have often said about my own situation. I have grown with the help of counseling, deep reflection, and being more self-aware. I work at all of these every single day. I am a better educator because of the situations I've experienced. I would, however, give all that up in a heartbeat to have grown up in a happy home and still have a family who loved me: a mother that I could call and get cooking advice or someone to congratulate me when I release a book, for example. The posttraumatic growth I've experienced gives me a reason for my childhood and a purpose moving forward. It does not excuse the trauma or eliminate the feelings and work I've had to do to get to my healing place.

## Secondary Traumatic Stress

As educators, we spend time in district-sponsored trauma-sensitive training that focuses on recognizing and supporting students who have been traumatized. While education, in general, is beginning to understand the importance of recognizing and treating traumatized students, there has been less of a focus on traumatized adults who work with students.

Secondary traumatic stress (STS), also sometimes referred to as compassion fatigue, can affect anyone, traumatized or not, who works with others who show symptoms of having trauma. Secondary traumatic stress is defined as, "the emotional duress that results when an individual hears about the first-hand trauma experiences of another. Its symptoms mimic those of post-traumatic stress disorder (PTSD)" (The National Child Traumatic Stress Network, n.d.). The PTSD symptoms that secondary traumatic stress will emulate can even appear in adults who have not experienced any kind of trauma of their own. Educators and other support professionals who tend to be particularly susceptible to secondary traumatic stress are those who are extraordinarily empathetic.

Because secondary traumatic stress can mimic PTSD, symptoms of it can be widespread and found in a variety of places in the affected person's life. Some common symptoms are (Administration for Children & Families, n.d.):

| Cognitive | Emotional |
|---|---|
| <ul><li>Lowered Concentration</li><li>Apathy</li><li>Rigid thinking</li><li>Perfectionism</li><li>Preoccupation with trauma</li></ul> | <ul><li>Guilt</li><li>Anger</li><li>Numbness</li><li>Sadness</li><li>Helplessness</li></ul> |
| **Behavioral** | **Physical** |
| <ul><li>Withdrawal</li><li>Sleep disturbance</li><li>Appetite change</li><li>Hypervigilance</li><li>Elevated startle response</li></ul> | <ul><li>Increased heart rate</li><li>Difficulty breathing</li><li>Muscle and joint pain</li><li>Impaired immune system</li><li>Increased severity of medical concerns</li></ul> |

## How to Cope

Secondary traumatic stress is more than just normal stress, and as with any mental health issue, the first course of action that needs to be taken to heal is to be aware of and admit to the possibility that it might be a problem. One might need to take some extra time out for him/herself to deal with the feelings. Practicing mindfulness and self-care, as discussed in Chapter 13, can help to alleviate the symptoms.

Also, if the effects of the secondary traumatic stress are too strong, knowing when to ask for help from a professional is important as well. If necessary, it's imperative to take time away from the situation and to recognize that for you to be the best person you can for your students, you need to be mentally and physically healthy which may mean temporarily removing yourself from the situation.

## Organizational Support

Districts can and should be a part of the support and healing process. Again, the first step in this support is awareness and acknowledgment of this different type of stress that educators may be enduring. The acknowledgment goes a long way in making educators feel "heard" (Treatment and Services Adaption Center, n.d.) and helps to destigmatize the feelings educators may be having.

The Administration for Children & Families (n.d.) has put out a Secondary Traumatic Stress Toolkit, which contains the following ways that organizations can provide additional support to personnel who are working with traumatized individuals:

- Create an organizational culture that normalizes the effects of working with trauma survivors.
- Adopt policies that promote and support staff self-care.
- Allow for diversified workloads and encourage professional development.
- Create opportunities for staff to participate in social change and community outreach.
- Ensure a safe work environment.
- Provide STS education to and encourage open discussion of STS among staff and administrators.
- Make counseling resources and Employee Assistance Programs available to all staff.

Allowing people to talk about their feelings and experiences normalizes what many may be feeling but struggle talking about. It's imperative that we create safe environments not only for our students, but also for our teachers.

## Trauma Squared

In cases where the educator has experienced trauma and subsequently works with students or other educators who are going through a traumatic event, they can be more likely to develop secondary traumatic stress. There is potential for the educator's traumatic memories or reactions to be triggered. Of course, as the stories in Part I have established, there is also the potential for the adult to have a better-equipped toolbox to help the student.

The results depend upon several factors including the extent of the processing of the traumatic event, the amount of healing that has occurred, the type and severity of the original trauma, and even the intelligence and self-awareness that the educator possesses. Multiple factors come into play when a traumatized teacher works with a traumatized student, but most importantly, the educator needs to be able to recognize when his/her attention needs to be on self-care and seeking out professional assistance if necessary.

Another way that secondary traumatic stress is similar to enduring a trauma or having PTSD is that we control how we choose to manage our situations and feelings. If we don't take the time to manage with self-care and seek additional help if we need it, we can't be the best people we can possibly be for our students. We are some of the people that they look up to most, and they will mimic our actions both good and bad, healthy and unhealthy. It's important that we be the person that we want to see in them and be reflective enough to know what we need to cope and heal. Taking a step on the path to healing is our choice.

# Chapter 15

# Control Your Ending

*Mandy Froehlich*

> *"You can't go back and change the beginning, but you can start where you are and change the ending."*
> -C.S. Lewis

Being an educator, by its very nature, is a deeply personal profession. Great teachers connect with their students on multiple levels and in a variety of ways. They form bonds. They celebrate birthdays, teach children to tie their shoes, and shake hands at graduation. They lie awake at night reflecting on an assessment that went awry, or over-excitement about a new lesson they're implementing. The personal nature of education is how it should be. After all, we are an integral part of shaping another human's life. For better or worse, a teacher can be one of a person's most prominent childhood memories.

Many wonderful educators have never had experiences like these mentioned in the story chapters. Similar to the teachers who have suffered a trauma, they bring their own type of special gifts to the classroom. They might understand having role models and supportive parents, and therefore know exactly how to bring those behaviors into their teaching. They might know how to create a warm, loving environment because that's what they experienced. There is the need for every kind of educator with all kinds of experiences working with our students. Our combined differences are what make us stronger as a whole. These educators' stories may not be represented in this book, but they are just as valuable and necessary.

Educator Mental Health

Education, in general, seems to be hesitant to acknowledge the fact that some teachers need additional support besides the typical mindfulness techniques they may be taught. These mindfulness techniques and training in stress reduction are fantastic and should be provided to everyone. For teachers who have not experienced trauma or have a mental health issue, mindfulness is an amazing way to reduce stress. However, with teachers who have additional needs, they need to learn mindfulness, but they also need additional assistance to be able to utilize the mindfulness to the greatest extent. With budget cuts and the greater need for student mental health services, supports in place to assist teachers with their mental health like Employee Assistance Programs, are considered a luxury when really, they should be a requirement; the baseline standard for everyone.

A Path Diverged...

Everyone has a story, and many times we have the choice of what path we want to follow. We make decisions that have natural consequences or that lift us up to bigger and better things. Sometimes, we are dealt a hand by someone else that leaves us with very little choice. But, the one thing we always have control over is how we react to circumstances.

What leads two children growing up in the same abusive home to lead completely separate adult lives: one following the path of the abusers; one diverging, learning the kind of parent they don't want to be, and becoming a kind, compassionate parent? Part of the difference is the choices each made and how they reacted to their adversities. In every situation, we can choose. We can allow adversity to make us bitter, angry people, or we can use what we learn to our advantage. In the cases of the people in these stories, they have chosen to utilize the strengths gained from suffering to not only become better people, but also better educators for the children they serve. They have recognized their posttraumatic growth and embraced the change. We may not choose to have had our challenging experiences, but we can choose to learn from them. Would we not ask our students to do the same thing?

The issue begins when we start to hide our traumas because we are afraid of being seen as "different" or "abnormal." This happens when we feel like the challenges we faced have made us weak or somehow inferior to others, or when we question if our experiences make us less of an educator. The problems continue if we hide any fallout from traumatic experiences and try (or are expected) to deal with subsequent mental health issues on our own.

But this, too, is another path we can take. Setting up organizational structures for support and awareness, such as the ones listed in the chapter, "After the Storm: Secondary Trauma and Post-Traumatic Growth," can help to break down barriers and destigmatize mental health issues and the stressors that accompany our profession. Our paths may include relentlessly pursuing these kinds of assistance through the district and leading the charge against ending the stigma toward mental health issues in your community. It's well past time to begin these discussions.

## Coping and Managing

Whether or not an educator has trauma in his/her past, there are ways to help cope and manage stress beyond mindfulness and self-care, even though I maintain that these techniques are extremely important for everyone to practice. These additional activities can create opportunities for support, growth, and reflection.

### Reflective Writing

Writing for reflection can be done in a number of ways. Sometimes people will keep journals or blogs for either professional or personal posts. Recently, my friend Michael Matera shared his professional video reflections that he has been posting on YouTube, which might work well for someone who may not enjoy writing or spending the time it can take to produce a blog post. The benefit of reflective writing or creating a reflective video is that it allows a person to get their thoughts down into some sort of format where they can reason through topics and issues, look for patterns once a few posts have been done, and most importantly, give themselves some "headspace" by organizing their thinking.

Even if the posts have nothing to do with the stressor, placing some of your thoughts into a medium you can revisit later will allow you to stop turning them over in your head, therefore freeing up space to evaluate other topics that may be causing you stress. A benefit of participating in these types of reflective exercises often is that the brain becomes accustomed to them, making it easier to reflect and organize thoughts the more you practice.

Currently, I choose to blog. If I am turning something over in my mind trying to reason through it, blogging forces me to get it written down. I need to make it a coherent thought in order to share it out, and that takes a significant amount of working through the issue. Once I have done this, I am able to stop thinking chaotically in my head and therefore, create some space. This is something I developed over time as I practiced effective reflection and putting my thoughts into writing. The ability to create that headspace has been what keeps me blogging.

**Growing your Support System**

Relationships should be the fundamental reason that we are in education. We are only as good as the people we surround ourselves with. Our PLN, our colleagues, and especially our students should make us better people. They should give us strength when it's

229

wavering and a high-five when something goes exceptionally well, just as we would do for them.

I have built my professional learning network (PLN) through social media and have taken time to meet people or connect with them either at conferences or via apps like Voxer. It takes time, no doubt, to maintain these relationships but anything worthwhile will take time. My friend, George Couros, always says that we make time for the things that are important to us. Relationships are the most important investment we can make.

I have worked hard to grow my PLN, and when it comes down to it, I have really amazing edu-friends. I know people who are very literally changing the face of education. They are caring, considerate, kind. They value students as I do, and spend energy helping others like I believe in doing. I have been fortunate to meet these people, but it's my desire to cultivate relationships that has kept me connected and continually learning from them. I do this by not only making time to listen when they are doing something incredible and want to share, but also when they need support, even if it's not advice they desire but rather just to vent. What I'm most proud of is when someone tells me they know they can count on me if they need me. That's how I know I've done my job in that relationship and it holds a very high value to me.

Creating a support system outside of work is important as well. In my experience, your family is not necessarily your blood relatives. Family members are the people you hold close, the ones who you know will support you and who won't look at you funny when you tell them you're struggling or suffering. They're the ones you can count on in times of need, your inner circle. It's important to know who these people are because if there's ever a time you really need them, you may not have the energy to wonder who will be there for you.

Also, in my experience, there is overlap between the people I hold dear and my PLN. These people are known as my Professional Learning Family (PLF), a term popularized by Sarah Thomas of EduMatch (ISTE, 2017).

This network of people I have created is what holds me up when I am struggling most. Some of them are so adept at knowing my eccentricities and mannerisms that they know when something is wrong before I even do, and they always know how I need to be supported. As I've stated before, they hold me up when I can't necessarily do it for myself. Finding these people before being put in a situation where it is imperative that you have support is critical. Whether the stress is personal or professional, you'll need a network in both areas to be a support system.

**Writing your Story through a Narrative or Poetry**

Writing about a difficult time, even if it isn't necessarily to the level of being a traumatic experience, can help clarify thoughts and feelings. Many of the contributors in this book had a difficult time beginning their stories. They were attempting, at first, to edit intense or extremely personal details out and thereupon developing a writer's block. They were also re-experiencing some of their more acute PTSD symptoms.

When this happened, I told them to stop writing their story for me and just to write. Write everything down and when they were done, burn it, tear it up, throw it away, whatever they had to do. I asked them to spew everything they had onto the paper (credit goes to my friend Kevin Honeycutt for this advice). Then, they were to go back to write their stories for me. In many cases with both the contributors and other people who wrote like this, writers found it to be incredibly healing and freeing. I was told it changed their outlooks, that it relieved pent up energy they didn't know they had. I had a contributor tell me that if I never picked his story, he didn't care because the process he had to go through to write it was so rewarding that it was enough. There is something incredibly powerful in watching your deepest fears and anguish show up as words on paper, and if it's something you truly desire to purge, lighting on fire and turning to ash, giving you back the control over your own story.

**The Fire Within**

Educators are amazing people. They chose to enter a profession where other people's children would be the top of their priority list. Typically, we discuss the importance of putting students first, as should always be the case. Sometimes, however, prioritizing students actually includes the act of an educator taking care of themselves both physically and mentally and knowing when additional help is needed.

I believe that educators enter the teaching profession with a fire of their own. You can see it in new teachers' enthusiasm to get into their first classrooms, their nervousness over meeting parents at back-to-school night, and the kind attentiveness they show their students. Their fire keeps them working late nights and spending hours reading blogs and Pinterest, looking for the next awesome lesson idea. However, if they don't take care of themselves as well, they will burn out. If they aren't aware, they could succumb to secondary traumatic stress if the conditions are right. All educators are in danger of this.

For those educators who have suffered adversity and trauma, it may have been our experiences that brought us to education in the first place. When healing has occurred, and there has been posttraumatic growth, our awareness becomes more heightened to what parts of ourselves we can use with students to provide them with the opportunities that make them desire to have to be the people they want to be.

Educators who have been traumatized may suffer from mental health issues and need additional support. They are not a group to be feared, nor should they feel ashamed. Instead, we should be supporting and accepting of their life lessons and the superpowers they've developed. It's those differences that have made them better people for our incredible students, and they deserve the very best we can offer.

### *I Am the Tree*
*By: Christine Lion-Bailey*

*A thunderous clap, a blinding lightning bolt*
*My heart, like an old tree, is severed in two,*
*Half still stands strong with roots firmly planted,*
*While the other half dies a slow death missing you.*
*My heart easily identifies with that big old tree*
*The exterior rough and weathered with pain,*
*Our branches extending to reach further out*
*To shelter everyone from the driving rain.*
*Always instinctually trying to protect*
*To bring safety and comfort to those who are near,*
*Focusing on others as a task of avoidance*
*Never needing to face my own sadness and fear.*
*Like the giant who lost its limb in the storm,*
*A critical piece that brings balance to the tree,*
*I lost my own sense of stability and security*
*Once I realized that you had forever left me.*
*For the longest time I wallowed in my sorrow*
*Feeling like I could never again be whole,*
*Like a piece of my heart had long gone missing*
*And I no longer was able to recognize my own soul.*
*Then one day the sun shone brighter than the clouds*
*Which constantly made life appear so dark and dim,*
*As I reflected upon this strange sense of warmth,*

# THE FIRE WITHIN

*I found a new motivation from deep within.
I slowly began to discover my repressed joy
Even when it felt like the darkest of day,
And I began a journey toward renewed happiness
Soul searching and aspiring all along the way.
I realize now that sadness is a blanket
Whose weight can be immense and difficult to free,
But when seeing all that there is to live for
I have found that great strength deep within me.
And so, I work to lift that cloak of sorrow
Seeing the light for which I am inspired to live
And I pray that if you are watching over me
Then it is a continued strength, to me, you will give.*

# Honorary Mention Student Poetry Submissions

The search for poetry submissions for the book began as a whim idea that was brainstormed due to the lack of open resource poetry in the theme that I was looking for. It turned out to be one of the best decisions I made for *The Fire Within*. The submissions I received were poignant, inspiring, heartbreaking, and honest. I had high expectations for the submissions and the winners, and they surpassed my expectations by leaps and bounds. Due to the number of amazing submissions I received and the sheer impossibility of choosing "winners," I decided to take an additional ten poems by students and include them for everyone to enjoy. I hope that it gives you a look into the hearts of some of our kids as it did for me.

## *Pain*
*By Sean Cortez (age 13)*

*The boy that everyone makes fun of,*
*He's poor*
*He's trying to support his family*
*Trying to get good grades*
*Trying not to get in trouble*

*The boy that has no problems,*
*He seems like a great guy in person*
*Inside he just wants to live a great life*
*At home he has an abusive family*
*His friends are his only escape from reality*

*Watching others in pain,*
*Is a terrible feeling,*
*Being a victim of pain is unforgiving,*
*Causing pain is traumatizing...*

*You help your friends in pain*
*And you feel great*
*But when you're in pain*
*"You're fine"*

HONORARY MENTION STUDENT POETRY SUBMISSIONS

### *Have You/Have I*
*By Emily Arruda (age 16)*

Have you ever looked in someone's eyes and seen glass?
Shattered into a million tiny pieces,
like it fell with a crash.

Have you ever checked and seen the marks
on a person's wrists?
Cuts and burns placed there
with no more than a hiss.

Have you ever asked someone how they're doing
and seen their face fall?
But they merely respond with
"There's nothing wrong at all"

Have you ever watched as a person began to cry?
And stayed there as they sat
Waiting for tears to dry.

Have you ever told someone
how much they mean to you?
But they look at you sadly because
They think it's not true.

Have you ever had eyes that crash
Into a million pieces
Like glass?

## THE FIRE WITHIN

*Have you ever let out a hiss*
*From putting burns and cuts*
*On your wrists?*

*Have you ever said "There's nothing wrong at all"*
*After someone asks you*
*And your face falls?*
*Have you ever waited for tears to dry*
*As you just sit*
*And cry?*

*Have you ever thought it's not true*
*When someone says*
*The important one is you?*

*I have.*

## Have You Ever
*By Cortlynne Froehlich (age 15)*

*Have you ever sat at the bottom of a mountain*
*And looked at it like you will never reach the peak*
*Or wonder how much you have to risk to try and climb it*
*Or maybe wonder if those risks*
*will even be worth it in the end*

*Have you ever climbed up a mountain*
*And dodged the falling rocks and debris*
*Or trip and fall just to sit down for a break*
*And stay there thinking the mountain*
*was simply too tall to climb*

*Have you ever smiled at the top of a mountain*
*And stared at the view from up above*
*Or remember all the times you thought of giving up*
*Or wonder what would have been different*
*had you not climbed that mountain*

*Have you ever sat at the bottom of a mountain?*

# THE FIRE WITHIN

### *Stuck*
*By Sydney Kreidler (age 13)*

*I'm still here*
*but no one seems to know*
*Like I'm invisible*
*I try to speak up*
*But no words come out*
*Like I choke on nothing*
*I try to raise my hand*
*But I don't move*
*Like I'm glued where I am*
*I'm stuck*

*You see me*
*But you don't talk*
*Am I even here?*
*I'm here banging on these walls*
*But you seem to never notice*
*Am I even here?*
*You've let it slip by for this long*
*What's a little longer*
*I'm stuck*

*I go to the world I want to know*
*Where you all aren't*
*I smell the salt*
*I see the joy*
*I see the bottom of the ocean*
*I hear the waves crashing*
*The dolphins jump*

## HONORARY MENTION STUDENT POETRY SUBMISSIONS

The splash takes me in with it
I fell the burning of salt running down to my lungs
I try to scream
But I don't
I'm stuck

I put the headphones on
A beat starts
A word escapes the singer's mouth
The music reminds me
But it's the only song I've been listening to
A soft, blue drip falls
I'm stuck

My legs feel heavy
I burn again
My eyes feel heavy
Another tear
My body cries in pain
I'm stuck

I want to scream it to someone
I want to feel magnificent
I want to not feel tortured every day
I want to feel love, compassion, life
But I only feel...
Stuck

I walk to the place it's most torturous
My head feels heavy
Another day forgotten

# THE FIRE WITHIN

*Another day tortured*
*Another day being invisible*
*I'm stuck*

*I come again*
*Day after day*
*I still feel the same pain*
*But one day it's different*
*I feel free*
*The sun shines brighter*
*The birds chirp louder*
*The song changes*
*The place is calming*
*The tears have evaporated*
*The pain is gone*
*Am I stuck?*

*A word escapes your mouth like the words of my song*
*I talk*
*Words flowing like words from our song*
*That glass wall that was once here is gone*
*I'm stuck*
*But stuck with feeling gold*

HONORARY MENTION STUDENT POETRY SUBMISSIONS

## **A Million Thoughts**
*By Dora Kara (age 12)*

A pencil, gripped tightly in my hand
The charcoal, gray lead dying my fingers as I write
As I spill my aspirations onto the page
All of the words surround me, they turn to blurs

My thoughts pour out of my head
They wrap around my neck, tightening
Doubts arise
I'm drowning in apprehension
I'm unable to find an ambition
I want to be saved

My eyes flutter open to an unknown scene
Have I been freed?
I'm close to completing a goal,
I reach out and close my hands suddenly
But as my hands slowly open,
Nothing is revealed

The goals slowly turn black
I turn my head to find a timer,
It runs out quicker as the goals darken
Vibrant achievements surround them
As I reach for one, the time increases,
I for once feel joy, I feel proud
But as I reach for a goal, I become overwhelmed
My vision shakes,
quiet mumbles are slowly flowing through my mind.

# THE FIRE WITHIN

*My head pounds*
*Whispers turn to yells*
*"Work harder"*
*A sudden scream*
*"Work harder"*
*The words overlap*
*"Work harder"*
*They all stop at once*

*The tears in my eyes dry*
*Slowly, I'm hugged by soft voices*
*"Relax"*
*A warm feeling runs through my body*
*"Relax"*
*I'm safe now*
*"Relax"*

*My weak body immediately strengthens*
*I recover to my regular self,*
*The only word that forces out of my lips is*
*"Happiness"*

HONORARY MENTION STUDENT POETRY SUBMISSIONS

### Everyone's Tears Matter
### but Yours Matter the Most
*By Anita Schaffer (age 14)*

*I'm cute on the outside*
*but dying on the inside*
*my tears don't show but I'm crying*
*I have a story that should be told*
*but who will tell it for me*

*tell my story I'll tell yours*
*you matter*
*you just don't think you do*

*trust me*
*you're important*
*to me*
*and others too*
*talk to me I'll talk to you*
*the only thing you gotta do.*

*is talk*

*say what you think*
*say what you want*
*no one can stop you from speaking your mind*
*give your opinion*
*it matters*

*make people listen to your story*
*show your smiles and tears it matters too*

### *The Hope Behind the Clouds*
*By Emaan Toseef (age 13)*

*Sometimes the clouds cover the sky,*
*And the rain begins to fall from up high.*
*Sometimes it gets real dark outside,*
*And wish you could go run and hide.*

*Suddenly, a bright line forms around the cloud,*
*And the heart and brain become quite loud.*
*The translucent sunlight shines right through,*
*Forming a rainbow with every hue.*
*You can climb up in life with a single rope,*
*Because look deep inside, there's your hope.*

HONORARY MENTION STUDENT POETRY SUBMISSIONS

## *Life*
### *By Brett Barnes (age 13)*

*Life can be like a camera;*
*Just focus on what's the most important,*
*And capture the good and most joyful times,*
*And if things don't go your way,*
*Just take another picture*

Life can be drama
Full of depression and distraught
Full of heartbreaking and hope
Full of misery and mournfulness
But in the end
There is always one good thought for 10 bad ones

Sometimes life is like a storm
You can choose to get swallowed in the center,
Stay away from the storm,
Or fight the storm

Life can also be like a roller coaster
Whenever there is a bump
You can choose to put your hand high and enjoy the ride,
Or you can scream until you cross the finish

### The Light
### By Jonathan Castro (age 13)

The excruciating pain of reality
is like being shocked by a live wire
Feeling the heat like a house set on fire
You only have one escape to be finally set free
You must find the light as bright as light can be

Flying over the past like the feeling of relief
But you must fly higher for the answers you seek
Looking down to the dark as you head towards the light
Congratulations, you survived another night

Everyone doubted you, said "you can't make it"
But when they've heard you got out, will they take it?
The words that they said took you into the dark
The live wire is dead, went out with a spark

So if you go down, do you think you'll get up?
So tell right now, do you think you have won?
The goal is right there, just reach out and grab it
Come on hurry up, it's time to commit
You did it
You made it out alive!
Let's go but continue to strive.

# References

Administration for Children and Families. (n.d.). Secondary Traumatic Stress. Retrieved May 21, 2018, from https://www.acf.hhs.gov/trauma-toolkit/secondary-traumatic-stress

Csikszentmihalyi, M. (1990). *Flow: The psychology of optimal experience.* New York, NY: Harper and Row.

Collier, L. (2016). *Growth after trauma: Why are some people more resilient than others and can it be taught?* Retrieved May 21, 2018, from http://www.apa.org/monitor/2016/11/growth-trauma.aspx

EduMatch. (n.d.). EduMatch Voxer Room 2. Retrieved May 21, 2018, from http://getconnected.edumatch.org/voxerrooom2

Guidelines for concussion/mTBI & persistent symptoms. Second edition. (n.d.). Retrieved May 21, 2018, from http://onf.org/documents/guidelines-for-concussion-mtbi-persistent-symptoms-second-edition

Heath, C. (2017). The power of moments: Why certain moments have extraordinary impact. Simon & Schuster.

International Society of Technology in Education. (2017). *Sarah Thomas on being a learner and building a personal learning family.* Retrieved May 21, 2018, from https://www.youtube.com/watch?v=lTqApfP_4ik

Kabat-Zinn, J. (2013). *Full catastrophe living.* New York, N.Y: Bantam Books.

McGonigal, J. (n.d.). *Live Gamefully.* Retrieved May 21, 2018, from http://www.superbetter.com/

Porges, S. W. (2009). *The polyvagal theory: New insights into adaptive reactions of the autonomic nervous system.* Cleveland Clinic Journal of Medicine, 76(Suppl 2), S86–S90.

Reivich, K., and Shatté, A. (2003). *The resilience factor: 7 keys to finding your inner strength and overcoming life's hurdles.* Broadway Books.

Saturday Night Live. (2013). *Penelope: Thanksgiving – SNL.* Retrieved May 21, 2018, from https://www.youtube.com/watch?v=w4maUKzCRCk

Strayed, C. (2012). *Tiny beautiful things: Advice on love and life from dear sugar.* New York: Vintage Books.

Taubner, S., and Curth, C. (2013). *Mentalization mediates the relation between early traumatic experiences and aggressive behavior in adolescence.* PSIHOLOGIJA, Vol. 46 (2), 177–192.

# REFERENCES

TED. (2012). The game that can give you 10 extra years of life [Video file]. Retrieved May 21, 2018, from https://www.ted.com/talks/jane_mcgonigal_the_game_that_can_give_you_10_extra_years_of_life

Tedeschi, R. G., & Calhoun, L. G. (1996). *The Posttraumatic Growth Inventory: Measuring the positive legacy of trauma.* Journal of Traumatic Stress, 9(3), 455-472.

The National Child Traumatic Stress Network. (n.d.). *Secondary Traumatic Stress.* Retrieved May 21, 2018 from https://www.nctsn.org/trauma-informed-care/secondary-traumatic-stress

The University of North Carolina at Charlotte. (2014). Posttraumatic Growth Research Group. Retrieved May 21, 2018 from https://ptgi.uncc.edu/

Treatment and Services Adaption Center. (n.d.). *TSA | Managing secondary traumatic stress for educators.* Retrieved May 21, 2018 from https://traumaawareschools.org/secondarystress

Van Der Kolk, B. (2014). *The body keeps the score: Brain, mind, and body in the healing of trauma.* Penguin Group, NY.

# About Mandy

Mandy Froehlich is currently a Director of Innovation and Technology and a Google for Education Certified Trainer, but has been involved in education in a variety of positions from teacher to technology integrator, and has also taught pre-service teachers educational technology at the higher education level. Mandy has presented nationally on technology integration, effective leadership, and building a culture and climate for learning. She also consults with state agencies and school districts on similar topics and maintains the educationally based blog Leadership, Innovation & Divergent Teaching.

One of Mandy's fundamental life beliefs is that people's stories shape who they are. Every decision, reaction, or relationship people have or create is directed and defined by their past experiences and how they have reacted to adversity. These stories also shape their engagement in their profession, and their love for learning and students. Her message inspires people to take charge of their stories and determine their own outcomes, and how to become re-engaged in the profession if that has been lost along the way. She has a special passion for bringing attention to the supports needed for mental health for both students and educators.

Mandy is invested in determining what needs to be done to launch an environment ripe for innovative change and divergent thinking. She believes that there are steps that can be taken to create conditions that give teachers the best chance to both be innovative and create opportunities for innovation for their students. She has devised a framework called the "Hierarchy of Needs for Innovation and Divergent Thinking" to assist districts to assess and implement systemic changes to support this thinking.

# Other EduMatch Books

Follow *The Teacher's Journey* with Brian as he weaves together the stories of seven incredible educators. Each step encourages educators at any level to reflect, grow, and connect. *The Teacher's Journey* will ignite your mind and heart through its practical ideas and vulnerable storytelling.

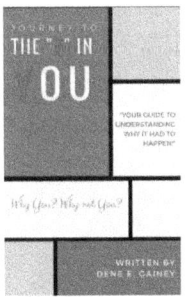

Why do you? Why would you? Why should you? Through the pages in this book, Dene Gainey helps you gain the confidence to be you, and understand the very power in what being you can produce. From philosophy to personal experiences, from existential considerations to the very nature of the human experience, consider who might be waiting on you to be you.

www.ingramcontent.com/pod-product-compliance
Lightning Source LLC
Chambersburg PA
CBHW052206090526
44583CB00017BA/2171